More Misused Words

No Mistakes Grammar Volume III

Giacomo Giammatteo

Copyright © 2016 Giacomo Giammatteo
All rights reserved.

Contents

Misused Words 1
Words 3
More Common Redundancies 27
Absolutes 47
More Absolutes 51
Words We Don't Need 55
How to Capitalize 59
Eponyms 65
Flat Adverbs 69
Initialisms and Acronyms 73
Latin Abbreviations 77
Words Difficult to Pronounce 87
How to Use Lie, Lay, Laid, and Lain 95
Poisonous or Venomous? 99
Plurals of Compound Words 103
Seventeen Time-Consuming Words/Phrases That Make You
Look Like an Ass (and waste your time) 105
Punctuation, (:!-*%;—@"-#,) and Other Things 111
Quotation Marks to Add Emphasis 115
Ellipsis 117
Parentheses—and when to use them 119
Closing 129

Other Books Coming Soon 130
Acknowledgments 133
About the Author 134

Misused Words

As always, I use this symbol—🐗—to indicate a tip or something important, so when you see that symbol, pay attention. Besides that, it's Dennis, my four-hundred-pound wild boar, and he would be unhappy if you didn't.

In this third edition of *No Mistakes Grammar*, I have once again spent a little time not only on misused words but also on redundancies, absolutes, eponyms, flat adverbs, acronyms, mispronunciations, and punctuation. I think you'll enjoy the diversity.

And once again, some of the material (such as mispronunciations) is a repeat from previous books, but it's because I felt the lesson was needed. If you feel you have a handle on it, skip that chapter. If not, take a refresher.

Words

Abjure/adjure
Unless you write historical fiction or fantasy books, I doubt you'll have much use for either of these words, but just in case . . .

Abjure—"to renounce or give up under oath."
After the wizard lost his powers, he abjured all titles or claims to power, choosing to hide out in a remote mountain village.

Adjure—"to command sincerely; to make a person swear an oath or threaten them with harm to do something."

During the Spanish Inquisition, the interrogators adjured the people to swear to the truth under penalty of death.

Acute/chronic
Some use *acute* and *chronic* interchangeably, but they have distinctly different meanings.

Acute means "sharp," but as in an acute care center, it's where you might take your child for an emergency. If you smash your finger with a hammer, it would cause acute (sharp) pain.

Chronic, on the other hand, means "long-term," as in "He suffered from chronic fatigue (long-term fatigue)." Or chronic back pain or chronic indigestion.

🐂 You might start out with *chronic* bronchitis and have a *chronic* cough, but the cough might cause you to break a rib, which would bring *acute* pain.

Acute can also mean other things, as in the measurement of an angle less than ninety degrees, or keen intellectual perception (especially of subtle distinctions), or acute hearing—the ability to distinguish the slightest sounds.

Adherence/adherents

Adherence—"the act of adhering, or showing allegiance," as in adherence to a political party. Or "stick to," as in adhere to the letter of the law.

Adherents—people who uphold a faction. Glue is an adherent.
The GOP has strong adherents.

Are/our

Are and *our* (and even *hour*) are often mixed up—and not just by English-as-a-second-language learners. It may stem from the way many people pronounce the words, though if done properly, there is a distinct difference.

Anyway, to get into the differences, *are* is a present tense form of the verb "to be." I don't like using grammar to explain grammar, so let's try some examples.

We are going to the mall.
You are her cousin.
Are you coming with us? (It's pronounced similar to the letter *r*.)
Our is a possessive. It is used to indicate ownership:
That is our car.
We just purchased our first house.
You are our friend.
Hour is a measurement of time equaling sixty minutes.

🐃 The easy way to remember this is that *our* with the *o* means ownership.

Attain/obtain
Obtain—"get something, an object, something physical."

Attain—"to reach a goal, put effort into acquiring something abstract."

He attained moral superiority.
She attained her goal of becoming a vice president by the age of thirty.

I've seen disagreement on the finer definitions of these words, with some stating that *obtain* means "to acquire through effort," but you can obtain anything in any manner. You might obtain a bottle of beer or a pack of cigarettes by buying it, yet it seems as if you must attain something (usually abstract) through hard work.

🐃 Remember that *obtain* usually refers to an object and that both begin with *ob*. On the other hand, *attain* usually refers to something abstract and both begin with *a*.

Auger/augur
An *auger* is a tool used to drill or bore holes. It can also be used as a verb, meaning "to drill or bore."

I have an auger on the back of my tractor. It's how I drill holes for fence posts. *Augur*—as a noun, "a seer or prophet." As a verb, "to make predictions, usually from omens or signs."

In ancient times, augurs were often consulted before important decisions were made.

🐟 Remember that an *augur* is a person and that an *auger* is a tool. So, you consult an augur and use an auger.

Avenge/revenge
Avenge—usually means "to inflict punishment" or "to mete out justice in retribution."

He avenged his son's murder by getting the killer convicted and sentenced to death.

Revenge—"to take vengeance or retaliate for injuries or wrongs that were either real or that you thought were real."

He committed murder to take revenge for his son's death.

Note: The best explanation for the distinction between the two is the quote by Samuel Johnson: "Revenge is an act of passion; vengeance of justice. Injuries are revenged; crimes are avenged."

Baited/bated
Baited—you can bait a trap or a (fishing) hook, or you can bait a person into a fight or into something illegal (or anything a person wouldn't ordinarily do).

She relentlessly baited him until he finally broke the law.

Bated—"to lessen the force or intensity of."
He waited with bated breath. (Not "He waited with baited breath.")

🐟 Remember that *baited* has the word *bait* in it, and you use bait to catch an animal or set a trap.

Bazaar/bizarre

A *bazaar* is a place where goods are offered for sale (often outdoors).

The church organized a bazaar to raise money for the homeless.

Bizarre—"unusual or not ordinary."

Her lip piercings, combined with her red and blue hair, presented a bizarre sight.

🐘 Remember that *bazaar* has an *a* in it, and so does *fair*. And *bizarre* has an *e* and an *i* and so does *weird*.

Bit/bitten

I overheard a friend of mine say that his daughter was bit by a dog the other day. It's a shame that the dog bit her, but she wasn't bit; she was bitten.

Without getting too technical, *bit* is the simple past tense, and *bitten* is the past participle and is used with an auxiliary verb, i.e., a helping verb. (Note that my intentional use of *i.e.* was to demonstrate that an auxiliary verb and helping verb are the same. Examples might better serve the point here.)

"The dog *bit* her." But . . . "She *was bitten* by the dog."

🐘 If there is a helping verb in the sentence, the word you are probably looking for is *bitten*. You can get a full list of helping verbs at wikipedia.com.

Born/borne

Born—"to be birthed or brought into existence."

The baby was born out of wedlock.

Borne—"transmitted by, as in malaria is a mosquito-borne disease." (Used in this sense, *borne* is part of a hyphenated word.)

Bring and Take/Come and Go

The basics of *bring* and *take* are simple. It all depends on location. You bring things here, and you take things there. So if you're at a location and you want something brought to you, you would say "Please bring me some food." But if you wanted to send some food somewhere else, you might say "Please take some food to Margie."

There are a few subtleties you may have to learn, but if you master this, you'll be right 99 percent of the time.

➟ You bring things here and take things there. You come here and go there. Remember that *take* and *there* both start with a *t*.

Callous/callus

Callous—"being indifferent or not sensitive; a person who shows no feelings toward others."

He was a callous sort and didn't care about his wife's misery.

Callus—a hardened patch of skin (usually on the palm of the hand). Calluses are often the result of hard work.

The callous farmer had calluses on his hands from plowing the fields.

Canon/cannon

Canon—a secular law or rule.

It is against the canons of the church for priests to marry.

Cannon—a piece of artillery (usually using gunpowder) that fires heavy projectiles. Examples of effective weapons are mortars and howitzers, which were used extensively during WWII.

Catalog/catalogue

This is one of the easy ones. *Catalog* is the US usage, while *catalogue* is UK.

🐦 If you can't remember it any other way, try to remember that the *e* at the end of *catalogue* stands for *England*.

Continual/continuous

These words have similar meanings. *Continual* is regular but with the possibility of interruption, whereas *continuous* is with no interruption.

Some people claim electronics technology has made continuous improvement, while others claim it has only been continual.

Continual noise often makes for a continuous headache.

🐦 A swift-flowing river might be said to have continuous motion, while a small creek might only be continual, such as when it rains.

Convince/persuade

Convince: to cause someone to believe that something is true.

The drugs he found in his son's room convinced the father he had a problem.

He persuaded his son to go into rehab, after the boy's second relapse.

🐃 Remember that you persuade someone to do something, and you convince that person *of* something. *Persuade* is for action, *convince* is only to make up their mind.

He might be persuaded to do that, but he will have to be convinced first.

Note: This word distinction is quickly falling by the wayside. Most people don't know the difference, and of those that do know, most don't care. If you're interested, learn it and stick with it. If you're not, I wouldn't worry about it.

🐃 Remember, you convince with facts and you persuade people. (Another one I use is "Scientists convince and salesmen persuade.")

Decimate

This is another word people seem to confuse. There are sides for and against the use of the word.

Many modern linguists support its meaning "to destroy/kill a larger portion of something." Other, more strict, linguists continue to use it only in the sense of "to kill one in ten," citing etymological reasons (the Latin root of *decimate*). Supposedly, an old punishment in Rome was to "decimate" a legion for a wrongdoing, in other words, to kill one in ten of them.

You are less likely to draw ire if you stick with the more classical meaning; however, there is probably enough evidence to support either position.

Decry/descry

Decry—"to criticize or condemn; to rail against something."

He wrote an opinion piece railing against (decrying) the new immigration policy.

Descry—"to detect something by looking or listening closely."
He descried a hidden agenda in the proposed bill, something he decried.

🐃 Remember that the *s* in *descry* stands for "see."

Note: This is not a set of words most people will confuse, simply because most people don't use them; however, if you're tempted to use either of these words, make certain you're using them correctly.

Drank/drunk

Many people confuse the use of these two verbs, especially if they drank a lot of liquor. *Drunk*, which can also be a noun, is easily identified when used as a noun. The confusion arises when people search for the proper past tense of *drink*.

Drunk can be used as a verb, adjective, or noun. Few people confuse it when used as an adjective or noun, as in "He's a drunk" or "She associates with drunk people."

But confusion sets in when we attempt to use it as a verb: "I *drank* the wine" and "He *has drunk* too much" are both correct. If you use the verb "to have" in any of its forms, use *drunk*. If it's the simple past tense of "to drink," use *drank*, as in "I drank beer after dinner" or "He drank all of the wine." But "I have drunk every drop."

🐃 Same as *bit* and *bitten* and *got* and *gotten*. If you use *have*, *had*, etc., use *drunk*.

Eminent/immanent/imminent/preeminent
Eminent—"used to describe a well-respected and renowned person, especially in a particular field of interest."

The eminent Dr. Henry Wells, a renowned biologist, will be speaking tonight.

Immanent—"restricted entirely to the mind; subjective" (*American Heritage Dictionary*).

Imminent—"something that will happen no matter what you do."

The attack was imminent.

Preeminent—"leading the field, ahead of the pack, superior."
He is the preeminent candidate.

🐗 Way to remember: "If someone is trying to appear eminent and uses the word immanent, you can rest assured it is imminent I will kick his preeminent ass." (This pneumonic device puts the words in alphabetical order.)

Enormity
Originally, *enormity* meant "of great evil—something wicked and bad;" however, it has evolved and is now commonly used to compare something great in size or scope—such as "the enormity of the project."

Many grammarians find fault with this, but it is more and more frequently used in this manner, so they (the grammar nerds) probably need to learn to accept it, as language is ever-changing.

Fervent/fervid

Though some grammarians say that there is a subtle difference, common usage doesn't bear that out. Both mean "with great passion" or "passionate" and are used interchangeably.

Neither word is used often, but when they are, you will be hard-pressed to identify a difference. So, if you have an inclination to use one, go ahead and do it. Either will work.

Flout/flaunt

This is one a lot of people mix up. You flaunt the new car you purchased, but you flout the law by running a stop sign with that new car.

🐗 Even after you learn the difference, it's difficult to keep it straight. I try to remember by using the "aunt" in *flaunt*. I pretend it represents an aunt who left me her wealth I'm now "flaunting."

🐗 The other way to remember it is to think of the "lout" in *flout* as a person who might "flout" the law.

Got/gotten

This is a pair of little words that causes a great deal of problems.

Got is the past tense of *get*, and *get* means so many things it's almost ridiculous. I've listed samples from dictionary.com.

Definitions for got (the definitions were from dictionary.com's website, but I selectively chose examples, which is why the numbering is odd.)
verb (used with object), *got* or (archaic) *gat*; *got* or *got·ten*; *get·ting*.
1. to receive or come to have possession, use, or enjoyment of: to get a birthday present; to get a pension.

2. to cause to be in one's possession or succeed in having available for one's use or enjoyment; obtain; acquire: to get a good price after bargaining; to get oil by drilling; to get information.
3. to go after, take hold of, and bring (something) for one's own or for another's purposes; fetch: Would you get the milk from the refrigerator for me?
4. to cause or cause to become, to do, to move, etc., as specified; effect: to get one's hair cut; to get a person drunk; to get a fire to burn; to get a dog out of a room.
5. to communicate or establish communication with over a distance; reach: You can always get me by telephone.
6. to hear or hear clearly: I didn't get your last name.
7. to acquire a mental grasp or command of; learn: to get a lesson.

verb (used without object), *got* or (Archaic) *gat*; *got* or *got·ten*; *get·ting*.
20. to come to a specified place, arrive, reach, to get home late.
21. to succeed, become enabled, or be permitted: You get to meet a lot of interesting people.
22. to become or to cause oneself to become as specified, reach a certain condition, to get angry, to get sick.
23. (used as an auxiliary verb followed by a past participle to form the passive): to get married; to get elected; to get hit by a car.
24. to succeed in coming, going, arriving at, visiting, etc. (usually followed by away, in, into, out, etc.): I don't get into town very often.
25. to bear, endure, or survive (usually followed by through or over), Can he get through another bad winter?
26. to earn money, gain.

noun
29. an offspring or the total of the offspring, especially of a male animal, the get of a stallion.
30. a return of a ball, as in tennis, that would normally have resulted in a point for the opponent.

31. British Slang. (A) something earned, as salary, profits, etc.: What's your week's get? (B) a child born out of wedlock.

Verb phrases
32. get about, (A) to move about; be active: He gets about with difficulty since his illness. (B) to become known; spread: It was supposed to be a secret, but somehow it got about. (C) to be socially active: She's been getting about much more since her family moved to the city. Also, get around.
33. get across, (A) to make or become understandable; communicate: to get a lesson across to students. (B) to be convincing about; impress upon others: The fire chief got across forcefully the fact that turning in a false alarm is a serious offense.
34. get ahead, to be successful, as in business or society: She got ahead by sheer determination.
35. get ahead of, (A) to move forward of, as in traveling: The taxi got ahead of her after the light changed. (B) to surpass; outdo: He refused to let anyone get ahead of him in business.
36. get along, (A) to go away; leave. (B) get on.
37. get around, (A) to circumvent; outwit. (B) to ingratiate oneself with (someone) through flattery or cajolery. (C) to travel from place to place; circulate: I don't get around much anymore. (D) get about.
38. get at, (A) to reach; touch: to stretch in order to get at a top shelf. (B) to suggest, hint at, or imply; intimate: What are you getting at? (C) to discover; determine: to get at the root of a problem. (D) Informal. to influence by surreptitious or illegal means; bribe: The gangsters couldn't get at the mayor.

Idioms
50. get back, (A) to come back; return: When will you get back? (B) to recover; regain: He got back his investment with interest. (C) to be revenged: She waited for a chance to get back at her accuser.
51. get even
52. get going, (A) to begin; act: They wanted to get going on the construction of the house. (B) to increase one's speed; make haste: If we don't get going, we'll never arrive in time.

53. get it, Informal. (A) to be punished or reprimanded: You'll get it for breaking that vase! (B) to understand or grasp something: This is just between us, get it?
54. get it off, Slang: Vulgar. to experience orgasm.
55. get it on, (A) Informal. to work or perform with satisfying harmony or energy or develop a strong rapport, as in music: a rock group really getting it on with the audience. (B) Slang: Vulgar. to have sexual intercourse.

As you can see, there are more definitions for *get* than you can imagine. Well, not quite, but there are a hell of a lot, and that makes understanding the nuances of the past tense confusing.

To top it off, there are exceptions to the norm, as in "I have got." It's usually shortened to "I've got," as it doesn't sound right as it stands, but then you have the expression (exception) "I have got to get out of here" (meaning "must," as in "I must get out of here").

To make matters worse, the UK version is different. In the UK, they say "have got" and consider it proper, while in the US we say "have gotten." All of this means if you do business on both sides of the ocean, you're bound to get confused more quickly.

Some people use "have got" to indicate ownership or possession, as in "I have got a lot of cousins," which means "I have a lot of cousins." So why not just say that? *Got* is not needed.

"I have *got* to go" (meaning "I must go"). You could also say "I have to go" instead and save yourself a word.

Gotten can mean many things. It can mean "to acquire or obtain," as in "I've gotten a new car." (You could also say "I've bought a new car.")

It can also mean "become," as in "I've gotten interested in art" (meaning "I've become interested in art"). Or "I've gotten confused by his politics." ("I've become confused by his politics.")

It can also mean "moved," as in "He's gotten out of the car" or "He's gotten off the sofa" (meaning he's moved off the sofa).

Much of the confusion can be cleared up simply by eliminating the words *got* or *gotten*. Examples follow.

Tim and his brother have got a snake. (What that means is that Tim and his brother own a snake.) You could just as easily say "Tim and his brother have a snake (or own a snake)."

An example using *gotten* would be "I'll watch TV later; I haven't gotten the dishes done yet." You could just as easily replace that with "I'll watch TV later; I haven't finished the dishes yet."

Not only did you get rid of the "gotten" problem, you saved a word while doing it.
Sometimes the easiest solution is the simplest, and in this case, I think the simplest is to substitute a word. Instead of saying "have gotten a dog," say "bought." Instead of "He got over his cold," say "He recovered." Instead of "She got caught," say "She was caught." If you do that, no one will misunderstand you, and no one can complain.

🐗 If you're going to use the words, though, try to do it right. If there is a helping verb, use *gotten*. If not, use *got* (same rule as *bit* and *bitten*).

Hopefully
This poor word has been beaten up badly, and I don't know why. It has long been used (and accepted) by almost everyone; in fact, dictionary.com had this to say: "Although some strongly object to its use as a sentence modifier, *hopefully*—meaning "it is hoped (that)"—has been in use since the 1930s and is fully standard in all varieties of speech and writing." (I put in the em dashes. Dictionary.com did not have them.) An example follows.

Hopefully, tensions between the two nations will ease.

This use of *hopefully* is parallel to that of *certainly, curiously, frankly, regrettably,* and other sentence modifiers.

Instant

Although *instant* has come to mean "quickly," or "instantly," it didn't always mean that. It originally referred to a precise, or specific, moment in time, as in "at the instant he passed" (that exact second) or "the instant I saw her, I fell in love."

Now it has come to mean "immediate" as in "instant coffee," or "I'll be back in an instant," or a mother admonishing her child with "Do what I say this instant."

Levee/levy

A *levee* is similar to a dam. It is a structure built to hold back water and prevent the land from flooding.

A *levy* is a tax or surcharge imposed upon a people or governed area. It could be money, food, soldiers, or anything.

The words are homophones, so they sound alike, and in normal speech it would be difficult, if not impossible, to distinguish the difference. In writing, however, it's easy.

🐦 Remember, *levees* are dams, and *levy* is a tax, and the *y* is next to the *x* in the alphabet.

Mask/Masque

A mask can be a disguise or a cover for the face. Masks are a common sight at Mardi Gras; in fact, to be unmasked would be unusual.

Someone might also "mask" his/her efforts in order to hide them.

Mask might also mean "to alter a photo."

Masque refers to a form of entertainment that appeared mostly in the 1500s and 1600s. The actors wore masks during the performances.

🐦 Remember, there are always masks associated with a masque.

Noisome

This is a strange word; not that many words aren't strange, but this one almost always throws me off track. Perhaps it's because of the pronunciation. It's pronounced as the combination of two words—*noise* and *some*, so you might think it has something to do with noise, but it doesn't.

Noisome means "objectionable to the senses," especially smell.

🐦 Remember that *noisome* has nothing to do with your hearing, but it does affect the senses.

Nonplussed

This word has been misused so often and so much that the wrong definition is in danger of replacing the real one, or, at least, being an alternative.

Nonplussed does *not* mean "not impressed." To be *nonplussed* means "to be confused, confounded, puzzled, etc." I doubt you'll ever have a reason to use the word, but if you do, rethink your word choice.

Penultimate/ultimate

Penultimate confuses many people. They think it means "the most" or "the ultimate," when actually it means "next to the last." It stems from the word *penult*, which means "the next to the last syllable." The problem is that many people don't know its meaning, so when they see *ultimate*, they assume (erroneously) that *penultimate* is even more than *ultimate*.

🐗 I don't see the public (not the general public) changing anytime soon, so my advice (not *advise*) would be to refrain from using the word—that is, if you're ever tempted to.

Plethora

Plethora does not mean a lot. It means "too many" or "an overabundance." An example might be—"The pond had a plethora of fish," meaning there were too many fish to live comfortably (or even too many to live). But you probably wouldn't say Baskin Robbins has a plethora of ice cream flavors (unless it was so many you couldn't make up your mind).

Poisonous/venomous

If you're ever on a quiz show and the question is "How many poisonous snakes are native to North America?"— the answer is none. A snake is not poisonous; it's venomous.

Certain tree frogs are poisonous. Some plants are poisonous. But anything that needs to bite or sting you to make you sick is considered venomous, therefore all poisonous snakes are actually venomous snakes. (There is one exception I know of. The Asian tiger snake is considered to be venomous *and* poisonous due to a diet of poisonous toads.) There has also recently been a discovery of a venomous frog in South America that has horns that jab you and deliver venom, hence it is a "venomous" frog.

🐘 It's simple to remember. Things that are poisonous need to be touched or drank, while venom needs to be injected.

Revert

To revert is "to return to a former state," not "to reply or respond to someone." An example might serve best.

He was loudmouthed and aggressive the night before, but this morning he reverted to his nondrunken, sober state.

After the drugs wore off, she reverted to the pleasant girl she normally was.

Reluctant/reticent

Reticent means "inclined to be silent or uncommunicative in speech," as in "He was reticent and wouldn't speak his mind."

Reluctant means "not willing to or afraid to do something," as in "He was reluctant to jump from the high dive."

You wouldn't say someone was reticent to perform an act. He/she might be reluctant, but not reticent.

Sit/set

Sit and *set* are similar to *lie* and *lay*; in fact, I often advise using them as substitutions to determine if the usage for *lie/lay* is correct.

You tell a dog to sit, as in "Sit, Fido." But you would *set* something on the table/chair, etc.

Just like *lie* and *lay*, *sit* and *set* require the same thing. *Set* is a transitive verb and requires a direct object, as in "You must set something (down)," whereas *sit* is an intransitive verb and does not require a direct object, so you or the dog may sit by yourself.

🐃 Remember, you can sit or *lie* on the couch, but you *set* or *lay* something down.

Sneaked/snuck
These words both mean the same thing—the past tense of the verb "to sneak." *Sneaked* is the preferred usage, though *snuck* is gaining ground. This is an irregular verb and, as such, is one of those that has to be committed to memory; it follows no rule.

So to speak
"So to speak" is used to indicate that the preceding sentence/statement is not necessarily literally true but perhaps in a metaphorical way, as in "The dog was his baby, *so to speak*." It means that the dog wasn't really his baby but he treated it as if it were.

Swim/swam/swum
This trio, though often confused, is easy to remember and get right.
Swim is present tense, as in "I like to swim." *Swam* is past tense, as in "I swam in the pond yesterday." *Swum* is only used with helping verbs, as in "She hasn't swum in years."

🐃 Helping verbs. Need I say it again? If you use a helping verb, use *swum*.

Theater/theatre
Same as *catalogue*, it's another US-versus-the-world situation. *Theater* is US, while *theatre* is UK.

🐃 Remember it the same way as *catalogue*. The one that ends with the letter *e* stands for *England*.

Tortuous/torturous
Something that is tortuous is twisting and winding, as in a "tortuous" climb up the side of the mountain, while something torturous is most likely painful.

🐃 *Torturous* is associated with torture. Remember they both have two *r*'s.

Trimester
A trimester is a period of three months. Some people think it means one-third (⅓) because the word *trimester* is typically used with things that last nine months, such as pregnancies or school years. But the word actually means "three months," so a year has four trimesters. It just so happens that a pregnancy and a school term have nine months, so a trimester equals one-third, making a trimester a convenient way to divide them up.

Ultimate
This is a word used to mean the last in a list; however, it is almost never used that way. It has come to be defined as "the best," "the most," etc., and seldom will you hear it used as originally intended.

Oddly enough, a closely related word, *penultimate*, is also misused, and in much the same way. *Penultimate* means "next to the last," as in "the penultimate chapter," or "the penultimate choice," but it has also been used as "beyond ultimate," or "better than the best."

I don't know how that's possible, but it has.

So don't fear if you misuse *ultimate* as an intensifier, Google will back you up. However, if you want to impress someone, use it the right way.

🐃 An easy way to remember the two is that *ultimate* begins with a *u* and *u* comes after *p*, just like *ultimate* comes after *penultimate*.

Note: I had planned on *ultimate* being the "ultimate" on this list, but unfortunately it will be "penultimate."

Whether (or not)

Courtesy of *Garner's Modern American Usage*: "Or not" is necessary when the phrase "whether or not" means "regardless of whether."

There are several complicated ways to determine whether to use "or not," but why be complicated? The simplest way to determine whether the "or not" can be omitted is to see if the sentence still makes sense without it. Here are a few examples:

I don't know whether (or not) I'm going to the concert.

If you use "or not," it makes no difference, so it's not needed. (You could also have used *if*.)

I don't know if I'm going to the concert.

But . . .

I am going to the concert whether she goes or not.

Now, try the sentence without the "or not," and you'll see it doesn't make sense—"I am going to the concert whether she goes" doesn't make sense, so the "or not" is needed.

More Common Redundancies

Everyone's goal should be to improve their communication skills, whether written or verbal. Both are called for in almost every job description you see, and the companies mean it. They want good communication skills (not communication*s* skills).

Redundancies are easy to overlook and are often skipped over even by a good editor; therefore, the burden lies on you, the writer, to get it right the first time. Learn to recognize the common mistakes.

Watch out for useless expressions, and cut out words that add nothing. Remember what Mark Twain once said: "I didn't have time to write a short letter, so I wrote a long one instead."

And he was correct. It's not difficult to sit at the computer and punch out keystrokes for a letter, but to edit it and make sure it sounds correct is something else entirely.

Below is a list of a few more redundancies. Some are repeats from the other *No Mistakes Grammar* books, but they're important enough to mention again. I've seen a few cases where the expressions were meaningful, but usually they bloat the writing. To improve your writing, simply eliminate needless words (the ones in parentheses).

Many thanks to Richard Nordquist at *about.com* for his examples of a lot of these redundancies.

Redundancies

Aid (and abet)

Since *abet* means "to aid," there is no sense in using it despite all of the cop shows you may watch. Remember, they are also the ones who issue "cease and desist" orders.

(All-time) record

If someone set a record, it already is "all-time," so no need to say it. "We've had *record* temperatures," means the temperatures were the highest (or lowest). Regardless of which, they set records.

Alternative (choice)

Choice is a synonym for *alternative*; in other words, it *is* an alternative, so no need to use it.

(And) etc.

It's covered under *etc.*, but I'll state it here. Since *etc.* means "and other things" or "and so forth," there is no need to use *and*. It would be like saying, "and and so forth."

(Armed) gunman

I think you can see the humor in this one. A "gun" man is already armed.

(Artificial) prosthesis

If a person has an artificial limb, it is known as a prosthesis. The definition of *prosthesis* is "an artificial body part."

ATM (machine)

An ATM is an automated-teller machine, so it's not necessary to use *machine*.

Autobiography (of his or her own life)

An *auto*biography *is* of your own life, told or written by *you*.

Bald (headed)
Bald refers to the head already. You can simply say someone is bald—you don't have to say *baldheaded*.

Balsa (wood)
Balsa is the name of the South American tree from which balsa comes. Since balsa is wood, there is no need to use *wood*.

Best (ever)
The best *is* the best. There is no sense in using *ever*.

Biography (of his or her life)
A biography *is* an account of someone's life written by someone else. If someone has a book written about them—it *is* a biography.

Blend (together)
Blend means "to mix." No need for *together*.

Bouquet (of flowers)
A bouquet *is* an arrangement of flowers.

(Burning) embers
Ember by definition means "burning" (the remnants of a fire).

Cancel (out)
I think this one is self-explanatory. You don't cancel out and you don't cancel in.

(Careful) scrutiny
Scrutiny, by definition, is careful. It means, the act of carefully examining something.

Cease (and desist)
I think detective shows are the culprit for spreading this misuse. *Desist* means "to cease." In fact, I believe *cease* is the first definition in most dictionaries.

Circle (around)
If you circle something (or someone), you are going around or surrounding it (or them).

(Close) proximity
Another cop-show misuse. *Proximity* means "close" or "nearby." Just say "He was in proximity to the crime."

(Closed) fist
To make a fist means "to close your hand."

Combine (together)
Combine means "to bring together."

Compete (with each other)
One of the definitions of *compete* is to try to win something that someone else is trying to win. In other words, you're *competing* for the prize.

(Completely) annihilate
Annihilate means "utterly destroy." Completely is not necessary.

(Completely) destroyed
Destroyed means "in total." If something was damaged, simply say so. If it was destroyed, it was *completely* destroyed.

(Completely) eliminate
Eliminate means "to get rid of" or "wipe out." No need to use *completely*.

(Completely) engulfed
If something is "engulfed," it is complete.

(Completely) filled
This one should be obvious. Think of a glass of water. Either it is filled or it isn't.

(Completely) surround
Surround means "to be all around someone or something." You could partially surround something but not completely, as *surround* already means all the way.

Connect (together)
If you connect or join two or more items, you are bringing them together.

(Constantly) maintained
Maintained means to keep something (even your body) to exist or continue without changing. So there is no need to use contstantly.

Could (possibly)
Consider this: he could ride a bike when he was six. In other words, he was able to. There is no possibly about it. He either could or he couldn't. Or someone is lying.

Crisis (situation)
The definition of crisis is: a difficult or dangerous situation that needs serious attention. Please note the word *situation*.

(Current) trend
A trend is current.

Each (and every)
You can pick *each* apple, or you can pick *every* apple, but not *each and every* apple.

Earlier (in time)
If it was earlier, it was already referring to time. Consider this: "I saw her earlier today."

Eliminate (altogether)
If you eliminate something, it *is* altogether.

Emergency (situation)
An emergency already is a situation, so no need to state it again.

(Empty) hole
A hole *is* empty. There's nothing in it!

(Empty) space
Same thing. A space *is* empty.

Enclosed (herein)
Herein means within a book or document, and enclosed means, well…enclosed. There's no need to use both.

Enter (in)
If you enter something, you *are* going *in*.

(Entirely) eliminate
Same thing as *completely*. If you eliminate something, it is in its entirety.

Eradicate (completely)
Same as *eliminate* and *engulfed*.

Evolve (over time)
Evolve implies a gradual change (meaning "over time"). Evolution doesn't happen instantaneously.

(Exact) same
Exact means the same.

(Face) mask
A mask is worn on the face. You don't wear an arm mask or a leg mask. If you say someone wore a mask, it's obvious where they wore it. You wouldn't say "He wore a face mask" any more than you would say "He wore a hand glove" or a "foot shoe."

Fall (down)
Where else do you fall? If you tell someone "He fell," they'll know what you mean. They won't picture you falling *up* to the roof.

(Favorable) approval
Approval implies a favorable response or action. Consider these: "He gave his approval" or "He gave his favorable approval."

(Final) conclusion
A conclusion is final.

(Final) end
The end is final.

(Final) outcome
The outcome is final.

(First and) foremost
Foremost (as the name implies) means "most prominent," so no need to use *first*.

(First) conceived
Conceive, meaning "to think up," (not as in "to become pregnant") means "to think of," so it's obviously the first time.

First (of all)
"First, let me say this," or "First of all, let me say this."

Fly (through the air)
Where else would you fly?

(Foreign) imports
If they're not foreign, where are they coming from?

(Former) graduate
If you have already graduated, then it is already in the past, therefore "former."

(Free) gift
A gift *is* free.

(From) whence
Whence means "from which" or "from where," so no need for *from*. It's similar to not using *and* with *etc*.

(Frozen) ice
I hope you see the humor in this one.

Full (to capacity)
Since *capacity* means "the maximum amount," there is no reason to say *full*.

(Future) plans
How many times has this interview question been asked? "What are your future plans?" A plan is always "ahead" of things; otherwise it wouldn't be a plan.

(General) public
The easiest way to show this is to provide definitions of both.

Public—of, relating to, or affecting all or most of the people of a country, state, etc.
General—of, relating to, or affecting all the people or things in a group, involving or including many or most people.

GOP (Party)
GOP stands for Grand Old Party.

Had done (previously)
If you already had done it, it was obviously previously.

(Head) honcho
Honcho implies "top dog," "leader," or "person in charge."

HIV (virus)
HIV—the *v* stands for *virus*.

(Hollow) tube
A tube is hollow.

Hurry (up)
What is the difference between *hurry* and *hurry up*?

(Illustrated) drawing
Illustrated implies that a book or magazine, etc., contains drawings.

Incredible (to believe)
Incredible is not an intensifier, as it is quickly becoming based on usage. It means "not credible" or "difficult to believe." A "credible witness" is one who is believable, but something "incredible" means the opposite. If you say

something is incredible to believe, it's like saying "It's difficult to believe to believe." Simply say it's incredible.

Indicted (on a charge)
Indicted means "charged."

Interdependent (on each other)
Dictionary.com defines this word as, mutually dependent; depending *on each other*.

Introduced (anew)
Introduced means "to bring something to the attention of others for the first time," so by definition, it would be new.

Introduced (for the first time)
Same as the previous example.

(Ir)regardless
Ir means "not," and *regardless* means "without regard." It defeats the purpose to combine them. Just use *regardless*.

ISBN (number)
We've been through similar situations before. The *N* in *ISBN* stands for "number," so saying "ISBN number" is like saying "number, number."

Join (together)
We've been over this before, too.

(Joint) collaboration
Same thing. A collaboration indicates it will be with someone.

Kneel (down)
How else would you kneel? Would you kneel up? Or sideways?

(Knowledgeable) experts
If they're experts, I would hope they're knowledgeable.

Lag (behind)
To lag means "to fall behind."

Later (time)
Same reasoning as before when we discussed *earlier*.

LCD (display)
More of the same. LCD stands for "liquid crystal *display*."

Lift (up)
Where else will you lift something?

(Local) residents

Made (out) of

(Major) breakthrough

(Major) feat

Meet (with each other)
Meet implies that there will be more than one person involved, whether it is for a lunch or dinner date, a business *meeting*, or a chance occurrence. So, if you tell someone, 'let's meet for lunch.' There is no need to add, 'with each other.'

(Mental) telepathy
Telepathy is "mind-reading," therefore it implies "mental."

Merge (together)
To merge means to bring together, or join.

Might (possibly)
Might is used to express the possibility of.

(Number-one) leader in _____
If you're the leader, you are number one.

Nape (of the neck)
Nape *is* the back of the neck.

(Native) habitat
Again, look at the two definitions:

Native—being the place or environment in which a person was born or a thing came into being.
Habitat—the natural environment of an organism; place that is natural for the life and growth of an organism.

(Natural) instinct
Instinct *is* what you do naturally.

Never (before)
If it was never, then it wasn't before either.

(New) beginning
A beginning *is* new.

(New) innovation
An innovation *is* new.

(New) invention
An invention *is* new.

(New) recruit
A recruit *is* new. You don't recruit old soldiers.

Nothing (at all)
If you have nothing, then you have nothing. You don't need to say "at all."

Off (of)
People say this frequently. "Get off of the couch." No need for *of*. "Get off the couch" will suffice.

(Old) adage
An adage is, by definition, old; in fact, some dictionaries refer to it as ancient.

(Old) cliché
By inference, a cliché, like an adage, is *old*. It couldn't very well be a cliché without having been around a while.

(Old) custom
Same as *cliché*.

(Old) proverb
Same as *cliché*.

(Open) trench
A trench is a ditch. The word became famous during the Trench Warfare of WWI, but regardless, a trench is open.

Outside (of)
The dog is "outside of" the fence. The cat is "outside" the fence. As you can see, it's the same.

(Over) exaggerate
Exaggerate means "to overstate" or "to stretch the truth." No need to say "over."

(Overused) cliché
Cliché means "overused."

(Pair of) twins
Twins *are* a pair.

Palm (of the hand)
Where else would the palm be?

(Passing) fad
A fad is short-lived, so it is always passing.

(Past) experience
Experience *is* in the past. So on your résumé, don't say "past experience." It makes you look foolish.

(Past) history
Same reasoning as *experience*.

(Past) memories
Same reasoning as *experience*.

(Past) records (not as in *feats* but in record keeping)
Same reasoning as *experience*.

Period (of time)
A period is *of time*. If not, then a period of what?

(Personal) friend
If they're not a *personal* friend, then whose friend are they?

(Personal) opinion
If it's not a *personal* opinion, then whose opinion is it?

Pick (and choose)
You can either pick something or choose something, but you can't do both.

PIN (number)
Same as ISBN, the *N* stands for number. You hear this one all the time. People say "I forgot my PIN number." If you do a Google search, you'll even see results from banks referring to it as a PIN number. They should know better.

Plan (ahead)
Same as "future plans"—plans *are* ahead.

(Polar) opposites
As in the North and South Poles—they're opposites.

(Positive) identification
If you ID someone, you are *sure* who it is, as in a fingerprint or DNA or dental records.

Postpone (until later)
To postpone *is* to put off (until later).

Pouring (down) rain
Which way would it pour?

(Pre)board (as with an airplane)
To *board* (verb) means "to get into or get onto," so how can you get on before you get on? That would be like the airline announcing, "Passengers can now get on before they get on."

(Pre)record
To record (as in *record*) is to write something down or save the digital (or taped) version of a voice/TV show/song, etc. You can't "pre" record something. That would be doing it before you did it. It would be like saying,

"Sue, record that song before you record it," or "Tim, write that down before you write it down."

Present (time)
The *present* is a part of time.

Protest (against)
A protest is an action or statement *against* something, like legislation. There is no need to protest "against" something; you simply protest it.

Raise (up)
Raise means "to move to a higher position," so if you don't raise *up*, where do you raise it?

RAM (memory)
Random access memory (an acronym) already contains the word *memory*.

Reason is (because)
A reason is "a cause or justification." He did it *because*. She couldn't go out *because* she felt bad.

Reason (why)
If you can tell me the difference between 'what was the reason he did it' and 'why he did it', I'll concede.

(Regular) routine
A routine *is* a sequence of actions that are *regularly* performed.

Revert (back)
If you revert to something, it means you go back.

Rise (up)
Duh.

(Safe) haven
A haven is a safe place. You've never heard of an *unsafe* haven have you?

Same (exact)
This is obvious. If something is the same, it is exact.

(Sand) dune
Dunes are made of sand.

(Serious) danger
Danger is serious.

(Sharp) point
A point is described as the sharp end of a tool, pencil, etc., so there is no need to mention sharp. The degree of sharpness might come into question, but *point* implies something sharp.

Skipped (over)
"We skipped the commercials," not "We skipped *over* the commercials."

Sole (of the foot)
The sole is the bottom of the foot. It's not a part of your hand or anything else.

Spell out (in detail)

Spliced (together)
Splice means to join together, as in he spliced the wires so they would work.

Start (off/out)
Consider: "The race started off with a bang" or "The race started with a bang."

(Sum) total
To sum something is to total it.

Surrounded (on all sides)
Discussed this already.

(Temper) tantrum
A tantrum is "a fit of temper." It is an uncontrolled outburst.

Three a.m. (in the morning)
See the section on dates and times. A.M. *is* the morning. There is no need to say it.

(Three-way) love triangle
Obviously, a triangle has three sides.

Time (period)
Talked about this.

(Total) destruction
See (completely) destroyed. Destruction is total.

(True) facts
By definition, facts are true—that's why they're called facts.

(Truly) sincere
Sincere is true.

(Two equal) halves
If a half weren't *equal*, it wouldn't be a half.

(Underground) subway
A subway *is* underground. The ones above ground are called "els," or "surface trains."

(Unexpected) emergency
I think it's apparent that an emergency would be unexpected. If you knew it was coming, you could prepare for it and it wouldn't be an emergency.

(Unexpected) surprise
Same reasoning as the previous example.

(Unintentional) mistake
I don't know of anyone who makes mistakes on purpose.

UPC (code)
Same as before. *Code* is included in the initialism.

(Usual) custom
A custom is usual.

(Very) pregnant
Don't make me laugh.

(Very) unique
Don't make me cry.

Visible (to the eye)
I prefer things that are visible to the ear or nose.

(Wall) mural
Since the definition of *mural* indicates location, what else would it be?

Warn (in advance)

If you *warn* someone, it *is* in advance of it happening.

Weather (conditions)

Write (down)

It would be silly to try it any other way, wouldn't it?

Absolutes

Many of you remember *The Princess Bride* and the Spaniard uttering his now-famous line—"You keep using that word. I do not think it means what you think it means." How can we ever forget Vizzini's (Wallace Shawn's) use of the word *inconceivable* or Mad Max (Billy Crystal) pronouncing the Spaniard's friend Wesley *mostly* dead, not dead? We laugh at the "mostly dead" reference, but we do similar things all the time. How many times have you heard the phrase "very unique"? If you've heard it once, it's one too many. And if you've said it, shame on you. Nothing can be "very unique," "very dead," "totally complete," or "absolutely perfect!"

List of Absolutes
- absolute/absolutely
- adequate
- chief
- complete
- dead
- devoid
- empty
- entirely or entire
- equal
- false
- fatal
- favorite
- finite or final
- full

- ideal
- identical
- immortal
- impossible
- inevitable
- infinite
- irrevocable
- mortal
- only
- opposite
- paramount
- perfect
- perpetual
- possible
- preferable
- principal
- right
- singular
- stationary
- sufficient
- unanimous
- unavoidable
- unbroken
- unique
- universal
- void
- whole

Let's discuss absolutes. There has been rampant misuse of absolutes the past few decades, and it seems to be getting worse. Hardly a week passes that I don't hear someone say "That was/is very unique." There are two things wrong with this statement.

1. You don't need the word very. (You seldom do.)
2. You can't use the word very with *unique*.

Unique means "one-of-a-kind;" therefore, intensifiers (words like *so, very, extremely*, etc.), are not only not necessary, they are not allowed. If something is unique, it's unique. It's not very unique or really unique. It's unique. It's already one-of-a-kind. It cannot be compared.

More Absolutes

Let's look at a few more absolutes, and there's no better one to start with than *absolute*. For as much as I hear "very unique," I hear "absolutely perfect" almost as much. I've even heard newscasters claim that something was "absolutely perfect," or "absolutely the best."

My question is, can something be more than perfect? If not, then how can it be absolutely perfect? Now, we're discussing two absolutes—*absolutely* and *perfect*, and there is no better time since *absolutely* is often used as a descriptor of *perfect*, even though it shouldn't be.

What other absolutes are there? Let's look at a few. This is not a comprehensive list, but it should cover the worst offenders.

Complete means "whole, having all the pieces or parts." So by definition, something is either complete or not. If it's *almost* complete, it's *not* complete. And if it *is* complete, it *is*. So you can't say something is *very* complete or *extremely* complete. You could say something is *almost* complete, but you could also say it is *incomplete*.

In the movie *The Princess Bride*, Inigo Montoya's friend Wesley (played to perfection by Cary Elwes) was pronounced *mostly* dead by Mad Max (Billy Crystal's character), but unless you're Cary Elwes, it's impossible to be *mostly dead*. You're either dead, or you aren't.

Things can't be the *most* impossible. They're either impossible (unable to be done) or they're not. If you have five tasks that are impossible, then you have five impossible tasks. None are more impossible than the others. If you have five difficult tasks, then they can, and will, vary in degree of difficulty, so you could justify saying, "This is the most difficult task" or something to that effect.

When dealing with absolutes, they are—for lack of a better word—absolute. In other words, it would be wrong to sit for dinner and exclaim, "This is absolutely the best lasagna I have ever eaten." It may be the *best* lasagna you've ever eaten, but it's not *absolutely* the best. It's either the best or it's not. (By the way, if it's my wife's lasagna, it *will* be the best.)

Absolutes, by definition, allow for no compromise. As an example, let's look at *empty*. In the sentence "The box is empty," it either *is* or *isn't* empty. There is no in between. If something is in the box, then it isn't empty.

The same goes for the word *all*, as in "He ate all the pizza." But what about this statement: "He ate nearly all of the pizza"? That doesn't tell us much, does it? If there were eight pieces of pizza, be specific, as in "He ate seven pieces of pizza." That tells us *specifically* how much pizza he ate. Try to be specific in your speech and especially in your writing. It makes for better communication.

This brings us to another one of my pet peeves, i.e., the misuse of *equal* or *identical*. Two things are either *equal* or they're not. If they're *almost* equal, then they are *unequal*. The same applies to *identical*. They call them *identical twins* for a reason—because you can't tell them apart.

Take a look at the rest of the list. These words are *not* to be modified. It was either a *fatal* blow or it wasn't. The evil overlord is *immortal* or he isn't. The universe is *infinite* or it isn't.

🐗 Remember, you don't have to be a professional writer to write better. I know plenty of people who aren't writers by profession, but they possess exceptional talent. Unfortunately, the reverse is also true. Something to practice is when you write—be specific. It may make the difference between *mostly dead* and *dead.*

Words We Don't Need

Any—Is It Needed?
If you read enough résumés or listen to enough conversations, you'll see/hear the use of *any* where it doesn't need to be. A primary example is the ubiquitous saying on responses to interviews: "Do you need any additional information?"

Take a look at that. Remove *any* from the sentence and see if it makes a difference. (I was going to say "and see if it makes *any* difference," but I caught myself.) Both sentences are asking the question "Do you need more information?" They mean the same thing, so *any* is not needed.

Both
"The wedding was *both* long and boring." Or should it be "The wedding was long and boring"? Did we need the word *both*? Did the meaning change? In the first example, you stated that the wedding was boring, and you endured it for an extended period. In the second example, you said the same thing.

Any
One, a, an, some, at all, all, more than one, in whatever amount/number/degree. It sometimes seems as if *any* can mean *anything*. But do we need it all the time? "Do you need *any* help?"—"Do you need help?" "Do you want *any* food?"—"Do you want food?" "Don't give him *any* money."—"Don't give him money." "Prayers didn't help *any*."—"Prayers didn't help."

Crutch Words

And other fillers or lazy words like *actually*, *basically*, *honestly*, *literally*, *uniquely*, *obviously*, and *like*. How many times have you heard people use these words as nothing more than fillers? And it's obvious, especially with *like*. *Like* may be the biggest offender of all, and while it seems to predominantly affect teenagers, it is prevalent in anyone who grew up in the eighties or nineties. And while I said *like* was the biggest offender, that doesn't ease the pressure on the other words to start pulling their weight. All these words are useful, but only when used properly.

"Tuna Fish" and "Safe Haven"

Tuna fish is one of those terms that has crept into the language, and, like it or not, it seems it's here to stay. But think about it. Isn't a *tuna* a fish? So why use both words? Can't you simply say "I'll have the tuna" or "I want tuna for lunch"? You wouldn't ask for *snapper fish* or *sea bass fish*, would you? No. You'd ask for *snapper* or *sea bass*.

So why is it *tuna fish*? When was the last time you heard anyone tell a waiter they would have the *salmon fish*? Is there tuna cow or tuna bird? One of the dictionaries listed *tuna fish* as "the flesh of the tuna," but I don't know if I buy that. No other fish is listed that way, so why *tuna*? It almost seems as if it's an afterthought. Do we need to distinguish the difference? And why not with other things? Do we say "chicken fowl," as in "I'd like a *chicken fowl* sandwich," or "I'd like six *chicken fowl* nuggets"? How about "What are you serving for Thanksgiving dinner?" "We're having *roast turkey fowl*. How about you?"

Safe Haven

Another thing that bugs me is *safe haven*. Do you know what a haven is? It is a place of shelter or safety. A place you can feel *safe*. So why do we need to say *safe haven*? Is this as opposed to an *unsafe* haven? *Is* there such a thing? If a haven is a safe place, then what is a safe haven? Is it a safe, safe place?

Maybe It's Possible

"*Maybe* it's possible." Maybe is *not* needed—simply say "It's possible." Look at these sentences.

"Are you going to the store?"
"Maybe." ("I might.")
"Are you going to the store?"
"It's possible." (Or "Possibly.") Unless you're trying to make an ass of yourself, get rid of the *maybe*.

How to Capitalize

When do you capitalize something? I wasn't going to include this until I realized that in the business world, especially on résumés, it is out of control. Look at any résumé you've sent and chances are it will have far too many words capitalized. It's as if the people are being paid for the number of capital letters they use. Capitals call attention to things, which may be why so many people overuse them—they want to focus all eyes on themselves. It isn't easy to know *what* to capitalize, but there *are* rules. Let's look at a few:

There is a definite trend toward *not* using capitals, so if you're in doubt and you can't refer to a style guide or ask someone, then scratch the capital. I promise—you won't get detention.

Two Basic Rules
Capitalize the first word of a sentence or the first word after a period.

This one is easy, and everyone should know it. It's not difficult to follow. If you are writing a sentence, capitalize the first word.

Capitalize proper nouns and specific geographic points/locations, etc.

We'll need a lot more space to go over proper nouns, as there are many rules within rules about how and when to use them. Geographic points and locations are easier. Let's try to cover that now.

If referring to a specific, named place, like the Sahara Desert, it's capitalized—as is the Nile River, the Desert Valley, or Lake Superior, but if you're speaking of the longest river in the world or the largest desert, then use lowercase letters.

The same applies to specific geographic regions. You would say "I'm from Northern California." but San Francisco is in the *northern* section of California. Or the Rio Grande lies in Southern Texas, but it is in the southern part of the state.

You might also say "I'm moving to the South. But you would say "I'm moving south." Also, "He was stationed in the Middle East, not middle east."

Specific events also get capitalized, like "The Napoleonic Wars," or "The War of Independence," or even the "Battle of Zama" (where Scipio Africanus defeated Hannibal in the Second Punic War).

Specific places that are man-made get capitalized also. An example: "If you go to New York, I'm sure you'll want to see the Empire State Building, just as you'd want to visit the Sears Tower in Chicago, or the Eiffel Tower in Paris."

Capitalization that many people struggle with is when to capitalize departments, or job titles, or a person they're addressing. Since these are such troublesome issues, let's try to tackle them.

The President
Everyone likes to capitalize *president*. Perhaps it's to show respect, though I doubt it. Usually it's because they have no clue when to capitalize and when not to. If you're speaking about a specific person, use a capital. Example—"The president will speak tonight." But, President Obama will speak tonight. They are referring specifically to President Obama, so it gets a capital. The same applies to dialogue. If you were to be addressing him and said, "Mr. President, I'd be delighted to attend," you would use a capital. But if the title

follows the name, you do not capitalize, as in, Barack Obama, president of the United States, will be there.

Dialogue

Suppose your mother's name is Margaret. Now try the substitution trick. "Mom, please get me some water." You *could* say "Margaret, please get me some water." But in this piece of dialogue, "My mom and I went to the store," you couldn't say "My Margaret and I went to the store." So in that case, *mom* would *not* be capitalized.

Departments

I'm not trying to beat a dead horse, but I do want to drive home a point and make it stick, so let's talk about job descriptions. Let's imagine "Bob" is your director of marketing and he accompanied you to a party.

When it came time for Bob to be formally introduced, you might say "This is Bob, Director of Marketing," but in an informal conversation with someone you'd say "By the way, we're looking for a director of engineering, as the previous one quit."

Bob got capitalized because he *is* the director of marketing. If your company is advertising for a position that needs to be filled, don't let them get carried away with capitalization. You're looking for a "vice president of sales," not a "Vice President of Sales." And you need a "director of mechanical engineering," not a "Director of Mechanical Engineering."

More on Titles

If a title precedes a person's name, capitalize it, as in "President Obama," "Governor Kelly," "Senator Krisp," but if it follows the name, leave it lowercased, as in "John Kelly, the governor of Nevada," or "Barack Obama, president of the United States."

Degrees and Majors in College

When it comes to degrees and the subjects a person majored in, there is a tendency to capitalize everything, but it's not necessary. If it's already a proper noun, leave it, as in "I majored in Latin (or English or Spanish)." But not *Economics*, unless it is the formal name of the course, as in "I majored in Economics 101."

Capitalize the names of specific course titles but not general academic subjects. So, to be specific, you would say "She received a BS in accounting—1992," or "I got a master's of science (MS) in engineering in 2000," or "He earned a PhD in biophysics—2007."

Job Titles

This is a tough one to grasp, and mostly because you'll see such variation. You should capitalize the name of a department only if it specifically refers to that department. Examples are below.

Joe works in the Marketing Department, Joe works in Marketing, but Joe works as a marketing analyst. (If it's the formal name of the department, you capitalize it, if it's the name of the discipline, you do not.)

It helps if you know specifics, as in "Joe is a director in the marketing department," but "Joe is *the* Director of Marketing." If your job is simply a function of the department, there is no need to capitalize, as in "Joe worked in business development for two years." If business development was a function in Marketing, then it would not be capitalized; however, if it was the name of a department (Business Development), then it would.

Trademarks

Since trademarks play a big part in business communication, let's address them. Many trademarks begin with a lowercase letter, such as iPad, iPhone, eBay, etc.

What do you do with them if they start a sentence? The accepted rule is if a lowercase trademark starts a sentence, keep it lowercase, as in, "iPhone sales went through the roof!" Or, "eBay's stock rose when it purchased PayPal."

Keep the second letter in caps, as that's how it's spelled, and we are only making adjustments to suit the rule about starting a sentence with caps.

Colons

Do not capitalize after a colon if you are writing a list, or if there is only one sentence following the colon:

John, we need the following: paper, pencils, pens, paper clips, and glue. (As you can see, nothing was capitalized.)

John, we need the following: it would be great to have paper to write with, as well as pens and pencils.
John, we need the following: It would be great to have paper. We also need pencils and pens, and paper clips.

The first and second examples required no capitalization, but the third—with two sentences following—did.

There are many more rules on capitalization, but it is too exhaustive a list to go into detail here. If you have questions, please email me.

Eponyms

An eponym is a person (real or fictitious) from whom something is said to take its name.

There are people who became so famous or achieved something so significant that they had a word, a permanent piece of the language, named after them. And it's not always real people either. Sometimes it's fictional characters that have become entrenched in everyday life.

I'm not talking about having a building, a road, a city, or even a state named after them but a *word*. So we're not speaking of things like the Kennedy Center, or the DuPont Highway, or Washington D.C., or even Pennsylvania, but real, live, everyday words.

Things like *sandwich, leotard, shrapnel,* and *erotica.*

Every day, people mention sandwiches. They eat them at home, order them at restaurants or at a work cafeteria, and yet how many people know where the word *sandwich* came from?

Sandwich—John Montagu, fourth earl of Sandwich and a British earl. He was a notorious gambler, and supposedly became so engrossed with his gambling that he wouldn't take time to eat, so he would instruct his aides/servants/valets to stuff some meat between pieces of bread, and he would satisfy his hunger in that manner.

Other people (gamblers) took notice and soon started ordering food, saying, "I'll have the same as Sandwich." The dish soon became known as a sandwich.

Shrapnel—Major General Henry Shrapnel was a British army officer whose name has entered the English language as the inventor of the shrapnel shell. When a bomb explodes or a grenade goes off and someone is injured or killed by the explosion, we say he was hit by shrapnel, but few people know why we say that or where the word *shrapnel* came from. Now you do.

Leotard—Most people know that a leotard is a skintight, one-piece garment for the torso, having long or short sleeves and a lower portion resembling either briefs or tights and worn by acrobats, dancers, etc. What many people *don't* know is that the leotard derives its name from Jules Léotard, a French acrobat who was one of the first to begin wearing what became known as the leotard.

Erotica—Most people know what erotica is, but did you know it derives its name from the Greek mythological character, Eros? (Also *eroticism*, *erotomania*, etc.)

There are hundreds more examples of eponyms. Here are but a few:

Achilles—Greek mythological character. From him we get "Achilles' heel" and "Achilles' tendon." He was supposedly invulnerable except in the heel, and at the end of the Trojan War, he was reportedly shot by Paris with a poisoned arrow (in the heel), thus giving us the name "Achilles' heel" as a weak spot or vulnerable place.

From **Adam** of the Bible, we get "Adam's apple."

From another mythological character, **Adonis** (a handsome young boy), we get *adonism*, "*Adonis* (plant)," etc.

We named the month of **August** after Augustus Caesar, the first Roman emperor, and **July** after his "uncle," Julius Caesar. We also get the words *czar*, *tsar*, and *kaiser* from Caesar.

The classical womanizer is known as a **Casanova,** after Gian Giacomo Girolamo Casanova, an Italian adventurer who lived during the late stages of the Renaissance.

We came to acquire the word *echo* from the Greek mythological character **Echo** and *floral/flower* from the Roman mythological character **Flora**.

Mentor was a Greek military strategist/tactician who fought against the Persians. From him we derive the term *mentor*.

Dame Nellie **Melba** was an Australian operatic soprano. She became one of the most famous singers of the late Victorian era and the early twentieth century. She took the pseudonym *Melba* from Melbourne, her hometown. Melba's name is associated with four foods, all of which were created in her honor by the French chef Auguste Escoffier:

- Peach Melba, a dessert made of peaches, raspberry sauce, and vanilla ice cream
- Melba sauce, a sweet purée of raspberries and red currant
- Melba toast, a crisp dry toast
- Melba garniture: chicken, truffles, and mushrooms stuffed into tomatoes with velouté sauce

From **Narcissus** we get *narcissism* (and *narcissist* and more).

From **Titan** we get *titanium*, and from **Uranus** we get *uranium*.

There are plenty more, such as the Gatling gun, a Beretta, the Diesel engine, the Ferris wheel, etc. but I'm sure you get the point.

Flat Adverbs

What is a flat adverb? Don't be embarrassed if you don't know. I didn't until about a year ago.

According to *Wikidpedia,* a flat adverb is an adverb that assumes the form of a related adjective, most often when words ending in *-ly* are used without the *-ly*. Though once quite common, flat adverbs have been largely phased out by their *-ly* counterparts. This shift is owed to eighteenth-century grammarians who insisted that adverbs end in *-ly*. Nonetheless, flat adverbs are preferred in some cases, as in "take it easy" and "sleep tight."

I found out what a flat adverb was by accident. I had given a first draft of my new novel to a group of beta readers, and a couple of them chided me for using *slow, fast, quick,* and *hard* instead of their normal adverbial counterparts (*slowly, quickly,* and *hardly*). In this case, *hardly* would not have worked, there is no normal counterpart for *fast*, and *slow* and *quick* sounded a lot better to me than *slowly* and *quickly*.

But was I wrong? I wondered, so I did some research. Here's what I found.

The first thing I found was that flat adverbs have been persecuted for a long time. The most famous of these, and one that drew considerable attention, was from an ad campaign Apple ran in the 1990s. It suggested that people *think different.*

Grammarians the world over raised a stink. "It should be *think differently,*" they said.

These grammarians were met by an even more vocal rebellion from the common people, who insisted that nothing was wrong with *different*. It turns out that the common people were correct. *Different* turned out to have been used as an adverb for hundreds of years, and the ad went on to become a tremendous success. Also, as a result of the initial uproar, many other flat adverbs were brought to light, including *bright, high, clean, slow, fast, quick, hard, sharp, soon,* and *tough*, among others.

Most of the criticism I caught was from dialogue (imperatives), and, oddly enough, that's where I found flat adverbs used the most. Examples follow.

- Drive slow.
- Be quick.
- Breathe deep.
- Hit him hard.
- Be kind.
- Run, Maria. Run fast!
- Aim high.
- Look sharp.

Let's look at how these would appear if we used their adverbial counterparts (where they have them).

- Drive slowly. (Not so bad—about the same.)
- Be quickly? (Doesn't work.)
- Breathe deeply. (Sounds the same.)
- Hit him hardly? (Doesn't work at all.) You could say "I hit him hard," or "I hardly hit him," but the meanings are almost opposite.
- Run, Maria. Run (fast)? (No counterpart.)
- Aim highly? (Doesn't work at all.)
- Look sharply. ("Look sharp" and "look sharply" have different meanings.)

As you saw with *fast*, some flat adverbs don't have a normal adverbial counterpart like *slow* and *slowly* or *quick* and *quickly*. A few examples are *straight* and *fast*. Others have counterparts but mean different things, as in *high* and *highly*. ("She thinks *highly* of him." "He can hurdle *high*.")

Let's look at a few sentences where we can and can't use them interchangeably.

Bright ✓
The lights of the city shine bright at night.
The lights of the city shine brightly at night.

Clean ✗
"You need to come clean," he said. Take note that you don't say, "You need to come cleanly." They are *not* interchangeable.
"Make sure and go to the reception cleanly groomed."

Deep ✓
"Breathe deep," the diving instructor told her.
"Breathe deeply," the diving instructor told her.

Hard ✗
He hit him hard.
He hit him hardly.

Fast ✗
Run fast, Maria.
Run (no counterpart. There is no 'fastly').

High ✗
Jump high, Tom.
Jump highly, Tom. (Doesn't work)
But, I think highly of him, does work.

Sharp ✓

He dresses sharp.
He dresses sharply.

You know the saying. "A little knowledge is a dangerous thing." Well, that applies here. Most people don't know if something is wrong with your grammar, but if they *think* it's wrong, you're likely to hear about it. And yet the flat adverb has been with us for a long time. Consider the expressions "He holds his cards close" or "Sit tight" or "Hang tough." Each of these words—*close*, *tight*, and *tough*—are functioning as flat adverbs, yet these sayings are used all the time, and accepted.

So, the next time someone tells you you're using the wrong word and they're referring to a flat adverb, tell them to go to . . . *here*.

Initialisms and Acronyms

The English language is full of redundancies, both written and verbal, so it's no wonder I've addressed this issue more than once. But this time it's different (at least I hope so). This time I'll be discussing a special kind of redundancy and one that has become prevalent in verbal communication.

Both acronyms and initialisms are abbreviations, but there is a key difference between the two. An *acronym* is an abbreviation formed by using (usually) the first letters of the words—and they *must* form a word, as in RAM (random access memory) or LASER (light amplification by stimulated emission of radiation), but an *initialism*, while formed the same way, does not have to form a word.

Examples of initialisms are:

FBI (Federal Bureau of Investigation)
CIA (Central Intelligence Agency)

Note how in these examples you say the word by using the initials. "F_B_I" or "C_I_A."

Style guides differ on whether to use periods, so I'll leave that up to you and your style guide. I'm not one to interfere.

One thing style guides seem in agreement with is capitalization. Both acronyms and initialisms are to be capitalized.

Initialisms and acronyms are great and save a ton of time. After all, it's easier to say LASER than light amplification by stimulated emission of radiation, or to say FBI than Federal Bureau of Investigation.

While all that is great, it brings another set of problems—our old friend redundancy.

Many of the abbreviations are prone to be redundant. Examples follow:

- ATM We addressed this before, but let's do it again. (automated teller machine) People say "ATM machine" when the word *machine* is already included in the initialism. That's like saying "automated teller machine machine."

- PIN Same thing, we've addressed it before, but it's prevalent, so let's do it again. (personal identification number)

    How often do you hear people say "I forgot my PIN number" or "I don't remember the PIN number"? Since *number* is already implied in the abbreviation—PIN—there is no need to repeat it. It's like saying, "I forgot my personal identification number number." Sounds pretty ridiculous, doesn't it?

    Despite this, hundreds of thousands of times per day, people are referring to PIN numbers. In fact, do an Internet search on "PIN number" and you'll be presented with more articles than you'd care to count listing it as such—many of them are even from banks.

- ATCS (air-traffic control system)

- SAT (Originally called the scholastic aptitude test, now it supposedly refers to nothing. Still, there is no reason to say *test*.) So it's not the SAT test, it's the SAT.

- UPC (No need to say UPC code, the *C* stands for *code*, as in "universal product code.")

- ISBN (ISBN number) Number is redundant.

- HIV (HIV virus) HIV suffices. No need for virus.

- VIN (VIN number) Same as ISBN. *Number* is not needed. Don't tell me you haven't heard people use "VIN number." I hear it all the time, even on TV when someone asks, "Did you get the VIN number?" or "Get the VIN number. We'll run it through the system." The problem is the same one as the previous example. Since *number* is already implied by the *N* in VIN, there is no sense in repeating it. It's like saying "Don't forget to check the vehicle identification number number."

There are plenty more to pick on, but I think you get the point.

Latin Abbreviations

E.g./I.e./Ergo/Et Al./Etc.
There are some people, especially those in the legal and insurance professions (as well as writers), who love to use Latin abbreviations. There's nothing wrong with that, but far too often I have seen them used improperly. The problem with using terms like this is if you're going to use them, many people won't know right from wrong, but of those who do, you'll look like an ass if you use them the wrong way. So, for those of you who would like to use the terms, here is the proper way.

e.g.
E.g. is a Latin abbreviation for *exempli gratia* and means "for example." It is not necessary to place it in italics, but you should write it with periods and lower case letters, and it is standard to follow it with a comma. Remember that *e.g.* should not be used for clarifying what you mean to say. Leave that job to *i.e.* Remember that *e.g.* and *example* both start with the letter *e*.

Working dogs, e.g., Great Danes, English mastiffs, and boxers typically like to be active.

Use *e.g.* when you want to give a *few examples* but not *a complete list*. As you can tell from the sample sentence, this is nowhere near a complete list. I could have added Bernese mountain dogs, Rottweilers, Doberman pinschers, and many more

i.e.

I.e. is a Latin abbreviation for *id est* and means "that is" or "in other words." It is used to clarify the meaning of something. It is written similarly to *e.g.* and is followed by a comma as well. It should precede a *clarification*, not an example. Use *i.e.* when you want to provide further explanation for something.

The fish expert recommended I only add aggressive freshwater fish to the tank, i.e., African or South American cichlids.

What follows *i.e.* should be equal to the thing it's clarifying, meaning you should be able to replace one with the other without changing the meaning of the sentence. Try it out with the sentence above.

The fish expert recommended I only add African or South American cichlids to the tank, i.e., aggressive freshwater fish.

Sometimes the situation would allow you to use *e.g.* or *i.e.*; however, the meaning of the sentence may be affected. Let's take a look at the above sentence. I said, "The fish expert recommended I only add aggressive freshwater fish to the tank." I then used *i.e.* to indicate that South American and African cichlids were what he was referring to.

If there were many choices, though, I could have use *e.g.* instead and still listed South American and African cichlids as examples. The difference is by using *i.e.*, I'm indicating that they are the only ones to use. By using *e.g.* I'm indicating they are but a few examples, that there are others that would work.

🐟 *E.g.* is used to *provide* an example and *i.e.* to *explain* an example.

; ergo,

Ergo is a Latin abbreviation for "therefore" and, as such, is frequently preceded by a semicolon. It can also be separated by a comma or an em dash, depending upon usage.

I see no need to use *ergo* but if you do use it, use it properly. This is from a blog I wrote, where I jokingly used *ergo*.

Perhaps they think that by capitalizing words, those words, or the functions they represent, become more important; ergo, the person becomes more important. (Did I just use the word *ergo*? I did, didn't I? Smack me if I ever do that again.)

, etc.

Etc., This is an abbreviation for *et cetera*, which means, "and so forth." It should never be used in the same sentence as *including* or *includes*, and it should be preceded by a comma and followed by a comma when it appears in the middle of a sentence. If it comes at the end of a sentence, the period (which is part of *etc.*) suffices as the final punctuation.

I've also seen people use "and etc.," which is also wrong as *etc.* means "and so forth," so the *and* is extraneous.

Some people may think the use of *ergo, et al., i.e.,* and *e.g.*, is pretentious, but the terms are perfectly fine and common practice, especially in the legal and insurance professions.

One other thing—*etc.* is used only for things. Use *et al.* when referring to people. (*Et al* means "and others," so it is appropriate.)

Etc. is used at the end of a list to indicate that there are more elements to the list being left out so that the list doesn't become too long.

All of the objects in our solar system (planets, comets, etc.,) orbit the sun.

When you use *etc.*, be sure all of the items that follow it are similar. For example, you wouldn't say "My passions are reading, writing, taking care of animals, etc." If you did that, no one would know what the *etc.* stands for as you have listed items of different kinds.

🐂 *Etc.* should always be used with items of the same kind, and you should never say "and etc."

Sic

I know you've seen this (usually in newspapers), where the author will cite a quote that contains an error in the original, then follows it with the word *sic*, in italics and brackets.

Sic is a Latin term and means "thus." It means this is exactly what the original quote or writing says, and it is used to let people know that an error was made and that the error was kept as it was by the writer.

Often it's a date, as in "America was discovered by Columbus in 1592 [*sic*]." The *sic* is needed as the date should be 1492, but the writer wanted you (the reader) to know that the person who originally wrote the article or said the quote did so erroneously.

🐂 *Sic* is always enclosed in brackets (one of the few times brackets are used) and is almost always italicized. So why use *sic* at all? Because a lot of statements, especially written ones, need to be copied word for word. It's not used to make the other person look bad.

Versus

Versus may be one of the most used of the Latin words/phrases, and yet most people don't know it's origin.

Versus means "against" or "as opposed to" and may be seen written as *vs.* or simply *v.* You've probably seen in the newspaper something similar to "Samuels v. the State of Texas" or (and I know you've seen something like this) "Patriots vs. Giants."

In each of these instances, you could have substituted *versus* for the *v* or *vs* without changing the meaning.

➤ *Versus* is used primarily when pitting one thing against another, as in "Patriots versus Giants" or "Samuels versus the State of Texas." In each case it signifies a fight or contest.

➤ It can also be used as a comparison, as in "pounds versus kilograms" when comparing the weight differences, or "yards versus meters," or "ounces versus liters."

Circa

This is another one of those Latin words I'm sure you've at least seen. It is often used in newspaper or magazine articles when the exact date of something is unknown, such as the construction or completion of an ancient project.

You may see something like "The completion of the Sphinx was *circa* 2500 BC." Another way to write it would be to say "The Sphinx was built about 4,500 years ago (*circa* 2500 BC)." In each case it means the Sphinx was built (about, around, or approximately) in the year 2500 BC.

et al.

Et al. is an abbreviation of the Latin phrase *et alii* (male), *et aliae* (female), and *et alia* (neutral gender), meaning "and others." The term references groups of people (not things). *Et al.* is useful for citations and for referring to a group by a few of its members, as in "The world was protected by mutants: Professor Xavier, Cyclops, Wolverine, et al."

Et al. is only capitalized at the beginning of a sentence, and it always takes a period. Commas are optional but typically used.

Quid Pro Quo

Most people understand what *quid pro quo* means, but they might not know what the literal (exact) meaning is.

Quid pro quo means "one thing in return for another." You often hear it referred to in talk of politics where one politician will do something for someone who has done something for them, although the spread of the word has far outreached politics and has become pervasive in almost all aspects of daily life.

A person's rise in politics is often the result of one quid pro quo after another. Many politicians rely on quid pro quo to get anything done.

Ad Nauseam

Most of you are familiar with the phrase *ad nauseam*. It means "to the point of sickness" and is used (mostly figuratively) that way.

We argued the point ad nauseam and still accomplished nothing.

Per Se

Many people use this expression, having picked it up through osmosis but never really knowing it's true meaning. *Per se* (not *per say*) means that something is being considered by itself—not with other things lumped into it.

The ex-alcoholic felt there was nothing wrong with drinking, per se, but that it must be done in moderation.

Vice Versa

Vice versa is another term most people know and which quite a few use. It means "the other way around," meaning if the statements were reversed, they would still be true.

An example might better serve the point.

During the Civil War, it was safe to say that people from the North did not like people from the South, and vice versa.

By using the term *vice versa*, we're stating that it's also safe to say that people from the South did not like people from the North. As we can presume that to be generally true, it's safe to say we used *vice versa* correctly.

Alibi

This is a word I never suspected to find on the list; however, it was there. Anyone who has ever watched a police show or read a mystery book is likely familiar with the meaning, but did you know it's Latin for "elsewhere"? "He has an *alibi*. He was *elsewhere* when the crime was committed."

We've covered a lot of ground, but we haven't even scratched the surface. There are hundreds, if not thousands, of Latin expressions/words we could have gone into. I'll bet you didn't know you knew so much Latin. Anyway, below is a brief list of the more common ones. We'll cover some more of them in detail at another time.

- *caveat emptor*—"Let the buyer beware." It's a warning to prospective buyers that they may be taken advantage of.
- ipso facto—"by the fact itself."
- veni, vidi, vici—"I came. I saw. I conquered."
- BC and AD—"before Christ" and "anno Domini (in the year of our Lord)."
- ad hoc—"formed or used for a special purpose."
- ad infinitum—"without end or limit."
- addendum—a section of additional material added to a document or a book, etc. (plural is addenda)
- affidavit—a sworn statement.
- alma mater—institution where one attended school.
- alter ego—technically it is a different version of yourself.
- alumnus or alumni—single and plural versions of graduates of a particular school or university. As an example: "He was a Princeton alumnus."
- ante bellum—"before the war" (especially the American Civil War).
- aurora borealis—Northern Lights.
- carpe diem—"Seize the day." It is a saying often used to urge someone to have fun while they can.
- cogito, ergo sum—"I think, therefore I am."
- e pluribus unum—I know you've seen this. It's on every dollar bill, written on the ribbon held by the eagle. It means "out of many, one" and is the motto of the United States.
- fac simile—means "to make alike" or "render a similar copy." As you may guess from the spelling, it is where the word facsimile comes from.
- persona non grata—an unacceptable or unwelcome person.

There are plenty more Latin phrases and words, but we'll save those for another time. Latin phrases are a part of the language, and they're not likely to change anytime soon, so it's better to learn the ins and outs while you can.

Words Difficult to Pronounce

There are some words that are difficult to pronounce. I'm not talking about the regional pronunciations you find, like the penchant for saying "wooder" instead of "water," which is common in the Baltimore to Philly areas, or the difference between crayfish and crawfish. I'm not talking about that.

I'm speaking of the mispronunciations of common (often imported) words. Which words am I speaking of? Let's look at a few from the list below. I've included links for each entry so you can hear how to pronounce them correctly.

- cache—You pronounce it "cash," as in the green stuff you carry in your pocket. You don't say "cashay."
  (*http://www.dictionary.com/browse/cache?s=t*)

- niche—It's "nich," not "neesh." Despite having French roots, the pronunciation is purely English.
  (*http://www.dictionary.com/browse/niche?s=t*)

- sherbet—This is one I've gotten wrong all my life. I've always said "sherbert," and it wasn't until researching this article that I discovered it to be "sherbet."
  (*http://www.dictionary.com/browse/sherbet?s=t*)

- arctic—It's "ark-tick" not "ar-tick (http://www.dictionary.com)

- Antarctica—The same applies. It's "ant ark-ti-ca" not "ant-ar-ti-ca." (http://www.dictionary.com)

- across—He doesn't live "acrossed" the street from her but "across" the street. I hear this mispronunciation frequently in common conversation. Remember—no *d* with an *a*. You might say he "crossed" the street, but that is a verb, not a preposition or adverb, and it has no *a*. (http://www.dictionary.com/browse/across?s=t)

- affidavit—People say "affadavid" all the time, but no matter how many times you say it, it won't be correct. The word is *affidavit*. It has a *t* on the end, not a *d*. (*http://www.merriam-webster.com/dictionary/affadavit*)

- ask—Some people think this mispronunciation ("aks") is restricted to poor, ethnic groups, but it's not. I've heard it said in formal business settings and even by a news announcer. It's one that shouldn't happen. The *s* comes before the *k* (http://www.dictionary.com).

- athlete, athletic—I've been hearing this mispronunciation since I was a kid. People continually say "athelete," inserting an extra *e* into the word. Try to remember that "athletes" *compete*, and both have only two *e*'s. (http://www.dictionary.com/browse/athlete?s=t)

- barbituate/barbiturate—Until I started doing research for this article, I mistakenly thought the proper way to say this was "barbiturate;" in fact, I thought that was the proper way to spell it also. Imagine my surprise to discover differently. (http://www.dictionary.com/browse/barbiturate?s=t)

- bob wire/barbed wire—When I first moved to Texas, I often heard people refer to that prickly fencing as "bob wire" or "bobbed wire." I wondered if it was different from the barbed wire I knew—wire that was barbed. Barbed wire is a noun phrase and is not hyphenated unless it functions as a modifier.

    His property is bordered by a barbed-wire fence.

He built his fence with barbed wire.
(http://www.dictionary.com/browse/barbwire?&o=100074&s=t)

- *calvary/cavalry*—*v* before *l*.
(http://www.dictionary.com/browse/cavalry?s=t)

- chomp at the bit/champ at the bit—"Chomp" has probably replaced "champ" in the United States, but we thought you might like to be reminded that the vowel should be a not *o* (http://www.dictionary.com)

- close/clothes—You wear "clothes," and you "close" the door. (http://www.dictionary.com/browse/clothes?s=t)

- coronet/cornet—If you are referring to the musical instrument, you say "cor-net." If you mean a crown, then say "cor-o-net." (http://www.dictionary.com/browse/cornet?s=t)

- diptheri/diphtheria—This is another one I have been mispronouncing for decades. I always said, "dip-ther-ia." Now I've learned that it is supposed to be "dif-ther-ia." Although now that I know how to pronounce it correctly, it will make it easier to spell, as the *ph* is a natural *f* sound. (http://www.dictionary.com)

- drownd/drown—I have often heard people use an extra *d* sound at the end of this. That's fine if you are referring to the past tense—*drowned*—but not the present tense, *drown*. So, for example, you would say "He drowned yesterday," but "He is going to drown"—not drownd. (http://www.dictionary.com/browse/drown?s=t)

- expresso/espresso—Being of Italian descent and loving espresso, it makes me cringe when I hear someone say "expresso," and I hear it all the time. Prior to the rise of Starbucks, I heard it much more often, but even today I hear it far too much. I even hear it from people who drink it—sin of all sins. It doesn't require much to get this right.

Look at the spelling. It has no *x*. Until they put an *x* in the spelling of *espresso*, let's pronounce it without one.
(http://www.dictionary.com/browse/espresso?s=t)

- excetera/et cetera—The same applies with *et cetera* (or *etc.*). There is no *x*, so don't pronounce it as if there were.
(http://www.dictionary.com/browse/et-cetera?s=t)

- Febyuary/February—This is a slightly different problem, though similar. People tend to pronounce *February* and omit the *r*, making it "Feb-u-ary." The "bru" is not the easiest sound to make, but you can do it. Give it a try. February is worth it.
(http://www.dictionary.com/browse/february?s=t)

- for all intensive purposes/for all intents and purposes—I don't know why this expression gets mixed up, but it does—greatly. And it seems to be the younger people who are mixing it up more. Think of what you're saying. *Intents* (meaning "intentions"), not *intensive* (meaning "increasing the force or emphasis (http://www.dictionary.com).

- forte/fort—The word is spelled "forte" but the *e* is pronounced only when speaking of music, as in a "forte passage." The words for a person's strong point/suit and a stronghold are pronounced the same: "fort." "Fort" and "fort-ay" are both now considered acceptable, though if you want to follow the older, more established pronunciation, stick with "fawrt" (fort).
(http://www.dictionary.com/browse/forte?s=t)

- heighth/height—This is the result of a common spelling error that lead to a mispronunciation. The way to spell it is without the *h* at the end. Perhaps there is confusion due to the spelling of *width* having an *h* at the end (and having it enunciated). *Height*, however, has no such spelling and therefore no such pronunciation.
(http://www.dictionary.com/browse/height)

- hi-archy/hierarchy—If you don't know this one, it's bound to trip you up, though it shouldn't, as it is pronounced as it looks—"hi-er-ar-chy." It couldn't be simpler, yet sooooo many people get it wrong. I always hear, "hy-ar-chy" (three syllables instead of four). I have to admit, my inclination is to say "hy-ar-chy." I have to stop and think to get it right. Do say "hierarchy."
(http://www.dictionary.com/browse/hierarchy?s=t)

- parenthesis/parentheses—Remember that if you place something inside of parentheses, there are two of them, so unless you are specifically referring to one, it's parentheses.
(http://www.dictionary.com/browse/parentheses?s=t)

I'm going to switch to a chart because some people learn better that way, and I felt that these words needed a little extra emphasis.

Word	What people say	What you should say	Listen here
jewelry	jew-ler-y	jewelry (say "jewel" then "ry")	(http://www.dictionary.com/browse/jewelry?s=t)
lambaste	lam-bast (like past)	lambaste (say "lam" then "baste")	(http://www.dictionary.com/browse/lambaste?s=t)
larynx	lar-n-yx	larynx (say "lar" then "ynx")	(http://www.dictionary.com/browse/larynx?s=t)
libel	li-bel	li-a-ble (libel is a different word)	(http://www.dictionary.com/browse/liable?s=t)

long-lived	long-livved	long-lived (rhymes with *alive*)	(http://www.dictionary.com/browse/long-lived?s=t)
masonry	mas-on-ar-y	mas-on-ry (there is no *a*)	(http://www.merriam-webster.com/dictionary/masonry)
miniature	min-it-ture	min-i-a-ture (four syllables)	(http://www.merriam-webster.com/dictionary/miniature)
nuclear	nuc-yu-lar	nu-cle-ar	(http://www.merriam-webster.com/dictionary/nuclear)
ordnance	ord-in-ance	ord-nance (two syllables)	(http://www.merriam-webster.com/dictionary/ordnance
prerogative	per-rog-a-tive	pre-rog-a-tive (remember, the *r* comes before the *e*, just like the beginning of *remember*)	(http://www.merriam-webster.com/dictionary/prerogative)
prescription	per-scrip-tion	pre-scrip-tion (same as the last one, the *r* goes before the *e*)	(http://www.merriam-webster.com/dictionary/prescription)
Realtor	Real-a-tor	Real-tor (do not add an extra *a*)	(http://www.merriam-webster.com/dictionary/realtor)
spay	spade	spay	(http://www.merriam-webster.com/dictionary/spay)

supposedly	sup-pos-a-bly	sup-pos-ed-ly (there is no *a* or *b* in supposedly)	(http://www.merriam-webster.com/dictionary/supposedly)
verbiage	ver-bage	ver-bi-age (three syllables)	(http://www.merriam-webster.com/dictionary/verbiage)
asterisk	as-ter-ick	as-ter-isk (don't forget the *s*)	(http://www.merriam-webster.com/dictionary/asterisk)

- ordnance—If you don't listen closely to the pronunciation, you might think is has three syllables, but a quick check with a dictionary will show you it only has two.

- spay—The confusion here comes from the pronunciation of the past tense of the verb *spay*. The past tense is *spayed*. So you would say "The vet spayed my dog yesterday, but the dog is at the vet being spayed" or "The vet will spay him tomorrow."

- verbiage—*Verbiage* has three syllables, although the mispronunciation (using two syllables) has become so commonplace that the original pronunciation is in danger of being lost. By the way, if you pronounce it properly, it will also help you remember how to spell it.

- ticklish, not tick-i-lish (http://www.merriam-webster.com/dictionary/ticklish)

- Illinois, not Ill-in-ois; say "Ill-in-oy." (http://www.merriam-webster.com/dictionary/Illinois) Same with *Arkansas*. Don't say "Ar-kan-sas" (as in "Kansas"); say "Ar-kan-saw."

- foliage—it has three syllables: "fol-i-age," not "fohl-age." (http://www.dictionary.com/browse/foliage?s=t) Some dictionaries cite the pronunciation with two syllables, but most use three.

How to Use Lie, Lay, Laid, and Lain

I don't know if I ever heard anyone use or even try to use *lain* in the proper manner; however, *lie*, *lay*, and *laid* are a different story. And no matter how many times we have been taught, the rules don't seem to stick.

I'm not saying I will make you remember; however, I may have a trick that will help.

First, let's tackle the rules (grammatically). The verb *to lie* means "to be in a horizontal, recumbent, or prostrate position." The opposite of stand.

The conjugation for *lie*: *lay* is the past tense, and *lain* is the past perfect. (More on conjugation later.)

Problems
Almost no one gets this right. Even idiomatic expressions (Idiomatic expressions are informal sayings that have a different meaning than the one expressed by the words. An example would be "Hold your tongue," meaning "Keep your mouth shut.") are wrong and are in danger of becoming entrenched.

Consider "Lie down on the job." It is more commonly known as "Lay down on the job." The even more common term "Lie low" has come to be known as "Lay low." If you say "Lay low," no one will look at you twice, but say "Lie low" and you'll draw more than a few sideways glances.

Further Explanation

If someone says to you, "The cops are looking for me. I think I'll lie low for a while," they would be grammatically correct but still in trouble with the law; however, if they said, "The cops are looking for me. I think I'll lay low for a while," they would be using the wrong word, but it would sound more natural. This error has come to such common use that most dictionaries recognize it as acceptable, and you hear it more often than not. This is a shame as it further confuses the *lie/lay* issue.

Tenses

The primary confusion of *lie/lay* comes because of the commonality of words. See table below.

|Tense: to lie | to lay |

| Present: lie | lay
| Past: lay | laid
| Past participle: lain | laid
| Present participle: lying | laying

Lie is an intransitive verb and doesn't require an object, while *lay* is a transitive verb and will be followed by a direct object. (A direct object receives the action of the verb, so the direct object will be whatever it is you're laying.) *Lay* means "to place some thing or someone down."

If you're like me, none of that means crap to you. You may as well be talking to the wall.

So what about the child's prayer "Now I lay me down to sleep"?

Since you are saying *lay me*, you technically have an object (Who are you laying? Me.), so grammatically, it is correct, though it might be damn difficult to lay yourself down. [sic]

How to Remember

It's easy to remember (he says with a cackle). After all, it's only taken me sixty years.

As we already know, one of the most confusing comparisons in the English language is the difference between *lie* and *lay*. It has long been disputed and has even longer been misused. How often do you hear anyone use it in the proper sense of "Yesterday I lay down for a nap"?

Probably close to never unless you hang out with a band of nerdy grammarians. Usually you'll hear "Yesterday I laid down for a nap," and no one bats an eye.

The correct way to say it is "I am going to lie down for a nap," or "I lay down for a nap yesterday," or "There have been days when I have lain down for two naps."

Write me a letter if you ever hear someone use *lain* that way, though, as it might be a first.

On the other hand, *lay* (when used as "placed") is typically used properly. "I am going to lay the pencil on your desk." Or "I laid the pen there an hour ago." Or "Yesterday, I had laid the eraser alongside the pen."

Remember this: you shouldn't use *laid* if it is in conjunction with sleep or rest unless it takes an object. So the statement "Yesterday I laid him down to sleep" is correct, but "Yesterday I laid down to sleep" is incorrect. In the first example, you laid someone (him) down to sleep. It has an object. In the second example, it has no object.

I told you I wouldn't expect you to learn grammar, but I lied—a little. The verb *lay*, as in "to place," requires an object; in other words, you need to have something to lay down. You can't tell someone to lay down or they have a perfect right to ask, "Lay what down?"

So don't be surprised if the next time you tell your dog to "Lay down," he asks you, "Lay what down?" You may be surprised that he spoke, but don't be surprised that he questioned your grammar.

Tip—Which Word to Use?

🐦 If you can substitute the word *place* for the word, it is usually *lay* (present tense), as in "Place (lay) the pencil on the desk."

If *placed* fits better, it requires *laid* (past tense), as in "I placed (laid) the pencil on the desk."

Not only does this method tell you if it works, it also indicates the tense (*place=lay* and *placed=laid*).

You couldn't say "I am going to 'place' down to sleep." Or "Last night I 'placed' down to sleep." It sounds ridiculous and doesn't make sense.

I'll say it again—substitute *place* or *placed*. If they make sense, use either *lay* (for *place*) or *laid* (for *placed*). If the substitution doesn't make sense, use *lie* for present tense or *lay* for past tense.

Poisonous or Venomous?

I know I've touched on this before, but I thought I'd expound.

For all of you writers out there—if you are planning to have your hero or heroine fall prey to a poison or venom, make sure you use the right word. If not, someone will pick up on it.

There was once a question on a quiz show—How many poisonous snakes are native to North America?

The answers ranged from zero to four to five.

The one who answered four was probably thinking copperhead, coral snake, cottonmouth (water moccasin), and rattle snake. I don't know what the one who answered five was thinking. But the one who had the correct answer was the contestant who said zero. She was correct because there are no *poisonous* snakes—at least not in North America.

The only one I am familiar with is the Asian tiger snake, which secretes poison from the toads it eats. This snake also is venomous, so it is one of the few animals that is venomous and poisonous. (Now *there* is a quiz-show question for you.)

There was another circumstance where an author used snakes as one of the key factors in their mystery novel. The author continually referred to them as "poisonous snakes" (though they weren't). After the first or second mention,

I became annoyed. Even worse, in the acknowledgments, the author even mentioned having consulted a herpetologist for advice. (The author should have found a better herpetologist.)

What's the Difference?

Despite what you may have heard all of your life, snakes (most of them) are *not* poisonous—they are *venomous*.

The terms *poison* and *venom* are often used interchangeably, but they have different meanings. It is the delivery that distinguishes one from the other.

I know, I know. This is getting picky. But if I'm reading a mystery and the author says someone was killed with a .45 caliber bullet when it was a .22, I'm going to be upset. There's no difference between that example and the poison/venom example. If it was venom that killed someone, I want to know. If it was poison, I want to know that as well.

Snakes, a few lizards, jellyfish, cephalopods, wasps, spiders, etc., inject venom, not poison. If you are bitten by a black widow, she injects venom into you. If you grab ahold of an arrow tree frog, or eat belladonna, or happen to have had dinner with Cesare or Lucretia Borgia during their heyday, then you are/were poisoned.

To set the record straight—if a substance is injected into you, as in bitten, stung, etc., then it's likely venom.

If you absorbed or ingested something, you were likely poisoned. (You might absorb poison by touching a poisonous frog, or you might ingest it by eating improperly prepared blowfish.)

To summarize the poison/venom comparisons, the following are the likely candidates:

| Poison | Venom |

arrow tree frog	snake (like rattlesnake)
belladonna	spider (black widow)
chemical substance	lizard (gila monster)
other plant	jellyfish
cane toad	lionfish

This is by no means a comprehensive list; in fact, it's pitifully short, omitting hundreds of poisonous and venomous creatures and plants. For a much more comprehensive list, see Wikipedia's article on poisonous plants and venomous animals at https://en.wikipedia.org/wiki/List_of_poisonous_plants, but don't let it scare you.

If you've been poisoned, you have either absorbed or ingested a toxic substance. A poisonous animal can only deliver toxic substances if another animal touches it or eats it. (Think of a poison dart frog or a blowfish.)

Venomous animals always *inject* their venom, whether that be by fangs (snakes or spiders) or stingers (wasps, bees, jellyfish, etc.).

As mentioned earlier, there is only one animal I know of that is poisonous and venomous—the Asian tiger snake. It earns this distinction because it is naturally venomous and gets its poison from its diet—poisonous toads/frogs. The poison is then secreted through the snake's pores and can be absorbed through touch.

The Asian tiger snake is unique; however, the Greening's frog is almost as rare. It is one of only a few species of venomous frogs known to exist. It lives in South America (where else?) and has venom-filled horns/spines on its head. The venom is so deadly it is said to be more potent than the venom produced by Brazilian pit vipers.

According to Carlos Jared, in a BBC article (http://www.bbc.com/earth/story/20150806-first-venomous-frogs-discovered), another frog that lives in the rainforest of Brazil known as Bruno's casque-headed frog has spines capable of producing venom twenty-five times more potent than the pit vipers. Calculations by Jared and his colleagues suggest that a single gram of the toxic secretion from a Bruno's casque-headed frog would be enough to kill more than three hundred thousand mice or about eighty humans.

I don't know about you, but I intend to stay away from frogs if I'm ever in South America.

There is one thing to keep in mind whether we're talking about venomous or poisonous creatures—with few exceptions, most of them are not lethal. And not all of the same kind are even venomous. Take the scorpion—of the more than one thousand known species, only about half a dozen are harmful to humans. And of venomous bites by copperheads, rattlesnakes, water moccasins, and black widows, more than 90 percent are not fatal.

We have had nine dogs bitten by copperheads, and not a single one died. One of the dogs (a stupid one) has been bitten five times. Now a bite to him is barely more than a bee sting—a testament to his immunity.

I hope you learned something from this. Not all snakes and spiders, etc., should be killed.

As a writer, I hope you also learned the difference between venomous and poisonous and that you'll use it in your writing from now on.

PS. During the past sixteen years, we have caught and relocated thirty-four copperheads, four water moccasins, and fifteen black widows. They were taken to a secluded spot in the woods several miles from our sanctuary.

Plurals of Compound Words

There seems to be a lot of confusion on how to pluralize certain words. Standard words like *moth* and *tiger* are easy; the plurals are made by adding an *s* to the end of the word, so they become *moths* and *tigers*.

But what do you do with words like *mother-in-law* or *attorney-at-law* or *major general*?

Some style guides say to pluralize the word that may change in number. In other words, using the examples above—and presuming you remarried—you *could* have several mothers-in-law, or if there were a convention for attorneys-at-law, you would have a hotel full of attorneys-at-law. The same applies for *major general*, though it would be *major generals*, as there would be a number of generals with the rank of major preceding their name.

The same logic applies to words like *sons-in-law* or *fathers-in-law*.

The number trick can fall apart when we have a word like *attorney general* as both *attorney* and *general* can be nouns and pluralized. So think of it this way. Imagine a room full of people and who they are. (Which are the nouns and which are the adjectives?) Are the people in the room generals who happen to be attorneys? If they are, then the word should be attorney generals, but more likely they are attorneys who happen to all bear the title of "attorney general," so collectively they would be referred to as "attorneys general."

"Major generals" would be the reverse, as they are generals who happen to have their title preceded by the term *major*, so for the same reason it's not "reds flower" but "red flowers," it's "major generals," not "majors general."

🐗 Remember, it's the one that can (*increase or decrease*) in number that gets pluralized. If that logic doesn't work, look for the important one, the noun.

Seventeen Time-Consuming Words/Phrases That Make You Look Like an Ass (and waste your time)

There are a lot of people who like to sound intelligent. There's nothing wrong with that, but they go about it the wrong way. They puff up their verbal communication and especially their written communication with flowery language and two-dollar words, when fifty-cent ones would suffice. In fact, not only would the fifty-cent ones suffice, they might sound better.

There are many particular phrases guilty of this. The following are seventeen of the worst offenders.

1. At a later time
2. During the course of
3. In order to/in order for
4. In the event of
5. Due to the fact that
6. At the present time
7. For a period of
8. Has a requirement for
9. In close proximity to
10. In relation to
11. In the amount of
12. In view of

13. In the process of
14. Is responsible for
15. The use of
16. Time period
17. With the exception of

Let's take a closer look at how a few of these wordy phrases may play out in normal writing.

With fluff

1. During the course of the meeting, you mentioned that at the present time you were swamped, and in order for you to get healthy, you'd need to rest for an undetermined period of time. (34 words)

2. The problem we have is that due to the fact that you're out, the marketing department has a requirement for an analyst, and in view of your situation, we are in the process of finding a suitable candidate. In the event of your quick return, we'd be willing to compensate you in the amount of $6,000 per month for the use of anything you need and for a time period of one year. With the exception of Margaret, who, as you know, is responsible for market research, this will make you the highest paid person in the department. (98 words)

Without fluff
1. During the meeting, you mentioned that you were swamped and you'd need to rest to get healthy. (17 words)

2. The problem is, because you're out, the marketing department needs an analyst, and due to your situation, we are looking for suitable candidates. If you return quickly, we'll pay you $6,000 per month for one year. Except for Margaret, head of market research, you will then be the highest paid person in the department. (55 words)

To summarize: The fluffy example took 132 words to write, while the concise version took 72 words. We saved 60 words *without* losing clarity. (Notice I didn't say without losing *any* clarity. That's because I didn't need the word *any* to make my point. I also could have said, "that's a savings of," instead of "we saved.")

Few people, if any, make all these mistakes, but enough of us are guilty of misusing *some* of them, and every word counts.

Every time you write something, look it over and ask, "Which words aren't needed?" and "How can I clarify this?"

Now that we've resolved that issue, let's look at the seventeen phrases and analyze them. First, we'll show what too many people say; then, in the table beside it, what they *could* say.

What gets said	Say instead	Example
At a later time	later	What's the difference between *meet me later* and *meet me at a later time?*
During the course of	during	*During the course of the movie*, he had to go to the restroom. *During the movie*, he had to go to the restroom.
In order to/for	to/for	He went to the store *in order to* get milk. He went to the store *to* get milk.
In the event of	if	*In the event of* a power failure, call the electric company.

		If power goes out, call the electric company.
Due to the fact that	because/since	*Due to the fact that* we have no power, we'll have to use candles. *Since* we don't have power, we'll have to use candles.
At the present time	now	I'm not conducting interviews *at the present time*. I'm not conducting interviews *now*.
For a period of	for	We'll have an interim CEO *for a period of* six months. We'll have an interim CEO *for* six months.
Has a requirement for	needs	The finance department *has a requirement for* an accountant. The finance department *needs* an accountant.
In close proximity to	near	The body was *in close proximity* to the river. The body was *near* the river.
In relation to	about or regarding	*In relation to* the lower sales . . . *Regarding/about* the lower sales . . .
In the amount of	use *for* or omit it	The charge was *in the amount of* $500.

		The charge was $500.
In view of	because of/due to	*In view of* her state of mind, we'll need a substitute. *Due to* her state of mind we'll need a substitute.
In the process of	omit (not needed)	He's *in the process of* painting the house. He's painting the house.
Is responsible for	does/handles or omit	He *is responsible for* buying the groceries. He buys the groceries.
The use of	omit	*The use of* the phrase "the use of" is not needed. "The use of" is not needed.
Time period	time	*During that time period*, I'll be away. During that *time*, I'll be away.
With the exception of	except	*With the exception of* Mary, we're all going. *Except* Mary, we're all going.

As you can see—I hope—from these examples, many of these words are not needed. The key is to recognize the ones you don't need and eliminate them or make substitutions. The easiest way of doing that is either removing the word/phrase or substituting another for it. If the meaning of the sentence changes, you have a problem, but if it doesn't, proceed.

Two of the worst offenders are "at the present time" and "in the process of." I think I hear these more than any, and they take up so much space. I asked a friend last week what he was doing, and he said, "At the present time, nothing." He could have just said, "Nothing." He wasted all those words for nothing.

And before you dismiss this advice as useless or nonsensical, remember, that snickering you hear behind your back may be coming from your boss.

Punctuation, (:!-*%;—@"–#,) and Other Things

I was going to wait and include this in the next edition of *Misused Words*, but then a few glaring errors on résumés captured my attention. The more I thought about it, the more I realized that the business world needed punctuation guidance, so I decided to include it in this version of the book as well as the next.

Punctuation

Have you ever tried watching a movie in the theater while people all around you are talking? Soon you are so annoyed you think of changing seats, or, worse, you start listening to the conversations. In any case, you are distracted, and if the movie demands close attention, you'll miss something important.

Now imagine the gatekeeper reviewing your résumé. She is cruising along, reading, getting into your background, when—wham!—misplaced punctuation takes her out of reading mode.

You don't want to distract the person reading your résumé, especially when they're at your work history.

The work history part of your résumé is the meat. It's where gatekeepers focus their attention. It's where you must avoid anything that makes them stop reading. Remember, a résumé's only purpose is to secure an interview.

Just like you wouldn't go to an interview with stains on your suit or dirt under your fingernails, you don't want your résumé to attract negative attention. It should be like a good interview suit—clean, the right size, and simple yet professional. You want to avoid all mistakes, even with punctuation.

I know that most people don't pay much attention to punctuation, but a misplaced comma or misused colon is as much a mistake as a ~~mispelled~~ misspelled word. If you're going to do a résumé right, learn to use punctuation, especially the dreaded semicolon.

Many people don't know how to use a semicolon properly. The solution is simple: if you're not sure how or when to use the semicolon, either don't use it or get your résumé checked by someone who does.

A Quick Lesson on Semicolons

There are three main circumstances when semicolons should be used. Despite what you might think, this isn't a grammar book, so I won't go into great detail.

- To join two independent clauses that are closely related.

John rushed to the store; he had to get milk and bread, or his wife would kill him. (See how the second clause is closely tied to the first? John's life depends on that first clause. The second clause explains why John had to rush to the store.)

- To separate lists that include commas.

John had fifteen minutes to do three things: fill the car with gas; stop and get milk, bread, and, perhaps a special treat; and get home before the new season of (take your pick) started.

- To join two clauses using a conjunctive adverb. (You see, that's why I didn't want to go into detail. Whenever I bring up conjunctive adverbs at parties, everyone walks away.)

John had three things to do; however, he decided to take a shower before doing them.

You shouldn't have to worry about most of this. About the only time you should need a semicolon in your résumé is for number two—lists that include commas.

Quotation Marks to Add Emphasis

Far too many people use quotation marks as a means to add emphasis to words or phrases when they should be using italics. Quotation marks *should* be used to cite a direct quotation, though.

The school principal said, "No school on Friday" during his announcement.

But you would *not* say

The principal declared Friday a "no school day."

You might, however, say

The principal declared Friday a *no school* day. (Or a no-school day.)

🐘 Use quotation marks for direct quotes or to indicate that someone is speaking, *not* for emphasis. You can also use quotation marks to indicate a word you are referring to, as in:

He asked what I meant by the word "ominous."

This lets readers know that what he asked about was the word "ominous." It is different than saying,

He asked what *ominous* meant.

Ellipsis

To start things right, let's get this out of the way—it is *ellipsis* (singular) and *ellipses* (plural).

An ellipsis is used to indicate words that have been omitted and, in most fiction writing, pauses in dialogue or narrator thought.

He wanted to tell her what he'd done, but . . .

I want to tell you what I've done . . . but I'm afraid you might get angry.

She was going to be married, but then . . .

Some style guides suggest no spaces either before or after the ellipsis or in between the periods. Most writing programs today have a feature that automatically converts three successive periods into an ellipsis, and most editors will accept that. (They do the same with two consecutive hyphens—convert it into an em dash.)

Parentheses—and when to use them

I'm guessing most of you know the way to use parentheses, but you might be surprised at some of the rules, especially the ones about how to punctuate them. Let's take a look.

The spelling of the word is the first thing to look at. *Parentheses* (with an *e*) is plural, and it's always used that way. This is different from ellipsis and ellipses.

Parentheses are used to indicate side remarks or to provide additional information. An example follows.

My black van (the one with the wheelchair ramp) has a handicap license plate.

Punctuation with parentheses is more complicated. The common usage is to place the punctuation *inside* the parentheses if it's a complete sentence.

I wondered where to take her to eat dinner. (Should I get Chinese food?) I decided I should just ask her.

If the parentheses end the sentence, place the punctuation *outside*.

He went north at the fork in the road (though he could have gone south). If the words inside the parentheses do not form a complete sentence, then place the punctuation *outside* the parentheses.

He came to a fork in the road and wondered (which way to go).

Commas almost always *follow* the parentheses also.

He came to a fork in the road (checked his map), then decided to head north.

One thing before we go further—whatever thought is within the parentheses should not be a primary part of the sentence. In other words, the sentence should stand alone. You should be able to remove the words inside the parentheses and have it still make sense (presuming it made sense before).

Other things to place inside parentheses include:

- The numbers of numbered lists, such as "Bring these items to the interview: (1) a résumé, (2) a portfolio showing your design work, and (3) a list of references."

- Area codes for phone numbers. We don't think much about this now as most smartphones and contact management lists format this automatically.

- Time zones, which are often cited in emails or other correspondence when arranging interviews. Example: "The flight leaves at 6:00 p.m. (EST)."

- To indicate a person's birth or death, as in "John Lennon (10/9/1940–12/8/1980), was a British (Liverpool) citizen and member of the rock band, the Beatles."

- To explain the meaning of, or to clarify, an abbreviation or acronym, as in "John Smith, the CMO (chief marketing officer) was just promoted again." You might also do the reverse. "John Smith, the chief marketing officer (CMO), was just promoted again."

It's only necessary to do this the first time you cite it. The rest of the time, the parentheses are not necessary.

Brackets

You may go through life and never have need of brackets, but then again, you may not. It would be great to know how to use them.

If you're quoting someone else but want to add clarification, use brackets.

I told Rose who we had lunch with, and she said, "Tom introduced us to Bob [his brother], but that's as much as I've met him."

You also use them to enclose the word *sic* or to make some other comment.

America was discovered by Columbus in 1592 [*sic*].

Em Dashes, En Dashes, and Hyphens

This isn't rocket science, but I thought I'd include how and when to use the different dashes.

What Is an Em Dash and How Do I Use It?

In order to understand an em dash, it's important to put it into perspective. That means we need to explore a few details on hyphens and en dashes. The following are definitions from *The Chicago Manual of Style*.

Hyphen

The hyphen connects two things that are intimately related, usually words that function together as a single concept or work together as a joint modifier (e.g., *tie-in, toll-free* call, *two-thirds*).

En dash

The en dash connects things that are related to each other by distance, as in the May–September issue of a magazine; it's not a May-September issue because June, July, and August are also ostensibly included in this range. In fact, en dashes specify any kind of range, which is why they properly appear in indexes when a range of pages is cited (e.g., 147–48). Note: You should use en dashes to separate the dates on your résumé.

Em dash

The em dash allows, in a manner similar to parentheses, an additional thought to be added within a sentence by sort of breaking away from that sentence. Em dashes also substitute for something missing. Also, the em dash may serve as a sort of bullet point.

The Most Common Uses of an Em Dash
Here are a few real-life examples of the three primary functions of an em dash:

- To take the place of a colon but with more punch.

Carla hated three things—deception, falsehoods, and lies.

- To offset a parenthetical phrase or thought.

No matter what happened—good, bad, or indifferent—in Uncle Dominic's house it was cause to put espresso on the stove.

- To indicate an interruption in dialogue.

"I'm through talking," he said. "The next time—"
"There won't be a 'next time,'" she said and slammed the door.

Bottom Line
To wrap this up neatly:

- A hyphen would be used to connect compound modifiers on a résumé, such as "hands-on manager," or "high-volume manufacturing."
- An en dash would be used to connect the dates on a résumé, such as "2003–Present."
- An em dash might be used in a cover letter. "As general manager—and temporary vice president of sales—drove profits to record levels."

Note: In all instances, you don't use spaces on either side of the dashes. (Some style books disagree.)

Technical Details

- To make a hyphen (-), press the hyphen key on the keyboard.
- To make an en dash (–), press Option+hyphen key on a Mac or, if using a PC, press Control+minus sign on the numeric keypad. If you don't have the numeric keypad, press Alt+hyphen key.
- To make an em dash (—), press Option+Shift+hyphen keys on a Mac or on a PC; press Control+Alt+minus sign on the numeric keypad.

Incorrectly Labeling Times

In almost any form of business writing or, for that matter, any form of writing, you will find it necessary to list a time, or times, in the communication. Here is the proper way to do it.

The interviews will be conducted between 8:00 and 4:00.

You would *not* say the interviews will be conducted between 8:00–4:00. If you use the words *between* or *from*, then there is no hyphen. If you do *not* use those words, then a hyphen is not only fine but required.

The interviews will be conducted 8:00–4:00.

This is a rule that isn't followed often, but it *is* a rule. If you want to look as if you know your grammar, stick to the rule.

Semicolons

I felt as if there was a need to further discuss semicolons, so we're going digging deeper here.

Some people swear that the dreaded semicolon is a monster and that it has no place in the modern world. I disagree. I think the semicolon has a few specific purposes and they benefit us all.

Below is a post I wrote about semicolons.

I'm Afraid of ;;;;;;

It's okay for writers to play with grammar. You don't have to write in complete sentences. Not all the time. Readers know what you mean because that's the way many people think.

Writers can put periods damn near anywhere. Well. Ma.ybe.

As the preceding example shows, you can't get away with putting periods after every word, and certainly not in the middle of a word, but choppy sentences in a novel are fine. Really. They are. You can even mess up with commas and em dashes or misplace the punctuation inside of the parentheses. Readers will assume you are taking liberties as a writer, and they won't worry about it.

Where you run into trouble is when you start messing with punctuation that most people don't know about. Or they only know enough to be dangerous. What am I talking about?

The Dreaded Semicolon

The semicolon is so feared that even editors are afraid of it. I recently had a writer tell me her editors steered her clear of the use of semicolons, going so far as to suggest that one per book could be too many. And Kurt Vonnegut was no friend of the semicolon. This is what Vonnegut had to say: "Do not use semicolons. They are transvestite hermaphrodites representing absolutely nothing. All they do is show you've been to college."

I'm not sure about the "transvestite hermaphrodites," but I'm pretty sure that was not a glowing endorsement.

So Why All This Talk about Semicolons?

I'm here to defend them. I've taken out my sword and drawn a line in the sand; I've had enough. Semicolons are magnificent little creatures that get no respect. Semicolons are like snakes; people fear them so they kill them.

I'm of a different mindset. I believe semicolons add a special flavor to a well-constructed sentence, a subtlety that a period cannot accomplish. A well-placed semicolon is precious—like a stolen kiss between secret lovers.

When You Should Use a ;

The most common use for a semicolon is to connect two closely related sentences. Think of semicolons like bridges. Imagine Manhattan if there were no bridges connecting it to New Jersey, or Brooklyn, or Queens, or the Bronx. That would make New York an entirely different place. Or suppose San Francisco had no bridge across the bay to Oakland. It wouldn't be thought of as San Francisco/Oakland anymore. It would just be San Francisco. And Oakland.

That's just one of the jobs a semicolon does; it connects two closely related clauses/sentences and brings them closer. Here are some examples:

- I can't eat past midnight tonight; I have to fast for a blood test tomorrow.
- I'm not working in the garden today; I saw a copperhead there this morning.
- Bob drove ninety miles per hour on his way to the hospital; his daughter's life depended on it.

In each of the examples above, there is a close relationship between the clauses, a relationship that couldn't be served by a comma and wouldn't be served by a period.

Another common use for semicolons is to clarify and separate a list.

In my book, *Murder Takes Time*, there are four main characters: Nicky Fusco, the hit man; Frankie Donovan, the cop; Angela Catrino, the love interest; and Tony Sannullo, the mob guy.

Let's look at that sentence if we used only commas.

In my book, *Murder Takes Time*, there are four main characters: Nicky Fusco, the hit man, Frankie Donovan, the cop, Angela Catrino, the love interest, and Tony Sannullo, the mob guy.

The second example, using all commas, is confusing. Using semicolons clarifies the meaning.

What You Don't Do with Semicolons
A semicolon should not be used in place of a colon. It's not a good substitute, and despite its name association, it doesn't want to be a colon. Semicolons are perfectly content doing the job they were meant to do.

A semicolon should not join two unrelated clauses.

Fear of Semicolons
I don't know why people are afraid. Look! ;;;;;;; They're not frightening; in fact, they're kind of cute. And it's easy to recognize not only what a semicolon is but what its function is. It is made up of a comma and a period. The period is on top, so your first inclination is to stop—as if it were a period—but then

you see the comma and continue. It couldn't be simpler. If you want to cast blame at the confusion surrounding semicolons, throw stones at the people who named it semicolon; it would have been better with a name like "periomma," or "commeriod."

The Bottom Line

Rise up, people! We've got to take a stand; the poor semicolon can't survive without us. And let's be honest—if we let the semicolon die, what will be next? The colon? Parentheses? Brackets? Pretty soon we'll be left with only commas, periods, and question marks. Some people may like that, but not me; I love my semicolons.

Exclamation Points

An exclamation point is similar to a jalapeño—one or two is fine, but too many are . . . well, too many.

There was even an episode of *Seinfeld* one time where Elaine, who worked at a publishing company, was editing a book, and there was a big argument over the use of exclamation points.

The bottom line is, they are used for extreme emphasis, and they lose all effect if used too often.

Exclamation points by nature denote surprise, anxiety, fright, etc. So there is no need to state that when in dialogue. I often see things such as:

"Call the police!" he yelled, or shouted, or screamed.

The use of the exclamation point already tells us that he uttered it excitedly. There's no need to tell us again.

Closing

In closing out this book, let me say thanks to all who read it. I hope you enjoyed reading it as much as I enjoyed writing it.

This book didn't come close to covering all of the grammar problems we're faced with, but if you run into any issues, feel free to write me. If I don't have the answer, I'll steer you to someone who does.

Ciao,

Giacomo

Other Books Coming Soon

Fiction

A Promise of Vengeance (Fantasy)
My first fantasy, and the first book in a four-book series—the Rules of Vengeance. (Three are already written and the fourth is being outlined.)

Murder Is Invisible ### (going through editing)
Frankie and Nicky are back.

Non-Fiction

- No Mistakes Grammar, Volume II, Misused Words for Business
- No Mistakes Grammar, Volume III, More Misused Words.
- No Mistakes Writing, Writing Shortcuts
- Uneducated—Thirty-Seven People Who Redefined the Definition of Education
- Whiskers and Bear—Volume I of the Life on the Farm Series (sent to editor)

Children's Books

- No Mistakes Grammar for Kids, Volume I—Much and Many (Sent to editor)

- No Mistakes Grammar for Kids, Volume II—Lie and Lay (Sent to editor)
- No Mistakes Grammar for Kids, Volume III—Then and Than (Sent to editor)
- Shinobi Goes to School—Life on the Farm for kids. (working on illustrations)

Get on the mailing list and you'll be sure to be notified of release dates and sales: http://eepurl.com/kS-IX

Acknowledgments

As usual I need to thank my magnificent wife, who has been with me much longer than she hasn't, but I also want to thank my niece, Emily, who has a magnificent grasp of the English language; in fact, she has been instrumental in helping me recover my speech abilities after having two strokes.

About the Author

Giacomo (Jim) Giammatteo is a headhunter and has done retained searches in the medical device/diagnostics & biotech/pharma industries for 30 years. He successfully completed more than 500 assignments, and he evaluated, edited, and wrote thousands of résumés. Giacomo has also interviewed and done reference checks on more than 1,000 candidates.

As if that wasn't enough to put him into a small room with padded walls, Giacomo is also a bestselling author of several mystery/suspense novels, including: *Murder Takes Time* & *Murder Has Consequences* in the Friendship & Honor series; *A Bullet For Carlos* & *Finding Family* in the Blood Flows South series; and *Necessary Decisions,* in the Redemption series.

His non-fiction work includes *No Mistakes Resumes* & *No Mistakes Interviews* Book I & II of the No Mistakes Careers Series.

In his spare time, Giacomo and his wife run an animal sanctuary with 45 loving *friends*—11 dogs, 1 horse, 6 cats, and 26 pigs. Oh, and one crazy—and very large—wild boar named Dennis who takes walks with me every day and happens to also be my best buddy.

Now that you've read the book, check out the website. Look around, click some links, and, if you've got time, tell me what you think. Contact me at jg@nomistakes.org

www.ingramcontent.com/pod-product-compliance
Lightning Source LLC
Chambersburg PA
CBHW070030040426
42333CB00040B/1421